FEDERAL REAL PROPERTY DISPOSITION

GOVERNMENT PROCEDURES AND OPERATIONS

Additional books in this series can be found on Nova's website under the Series tab.

Additional E-books in this series can be found on Nova's website under the E-book tab.

GOVERNMENT PROCEDURES AND OPERATIONS

FEDERAL REAL PROPERTY DISPOSITION

IAIN D. HAQUE
EDITOR

Nova Science Publishers, Inc.
New York

For permission to use material from this book please contact us:
Telephone 631-231-7269; Fax 631-231-8175
Web Site: http://www.novapublishers.com

NOTICE TO THE READER

The Publisher has taken reasonable care in the preparation of this book, but makes no expressed or implied warranty of any kind and assumes no responsibility for any errors or omissions. No liability is assumed for incidental or consequential damages in connection with or arising out of information contained in this book. The Publisher shall not be liable for any special, consequential, or exemplary damages resulting, in whole or in part, from the readers' use of, or reliance upon, this material. Any parts of this book based on government reports are so indicated and copyright is claimed for those parts to the extent applicable to compilations of such works.

Independent verification should be sought for any data, advice or recommendations contained in this book. In addition, no responsibility is assumed by the publisher for any injury and/or damage to persons or property arising from any methods, products, instructions, ideas or otherwise contained in this publication.

This publication is designed to provide accurate and authoritative information with regard to the subject matter covered herein. It is sold with the clear understanding that the Publisher is not engaged in rendering legal or any other professional services. If legal or any other expert assistance is required, the services of a competent person should be sought. FROM A DECLARATION OF PARTICIPANTS JOINTLY ADOPTED BY A COMMITTEE OF THE AMERICAN BAR ASSOCIATION AND A COMMITTEE OF PUBLISHERS.

Additional color graphics may be available in the e-book version of this book.

Library of Congress Cataloging-in-Publication Data
Federal real property disposition / editor, Iain D. Haque.
    p. cm.
  Includes index.
  ISBN 978-1-62100-048-8 (hardcover)
  1. Government property--United States. 2. Surplus government property--United States. 3.
Government sale of real property--United States. 4. Government property--United States--Purchasing.
5. Surplus government property--United States--Purchasing. I. Haque, Iain D.
  JK1661.F43 2011   352.5'4--dc23   2011029483

Published by Nova Science Publishers, Inc. † *New York*

CONTENTS

PREFACE

This book begins with an explanation of the real property disposal process and then discusses some of the factors that have made disposition inefficient and costly. Discussed also are real property legislation introduced in the 111th Congress that would address these problems and policy options for enhancing both the disposal process and congressional oversight.

Chapter 1- Federal executive branch agencies hold an extensive real property portfolio that includes nearly 900,000 buildings and structures, and 41 million acres of land worldwide. These assets have been acquired over a period of decades to help agencies fulfill their diverse missions. The government's portfolio encompasses properties with a range of uses, including barracks, health clinics, warehouses, laboratories, national parks, boat docks, and offices. As agencies' missions change over time, so, too, do their real property needs, thereby rendering some assets less useful or unneeded altogether.

Chapter 2- The federal government holds more than 45,000 underutilized properties that cost nearly $1.7 billion annually to operate, yet significant obstacles impede efforts to close, consolidate, or find other uses for these properties. GAO has designated federal real property management as a high-risk area, in part because of the number and cost of these properties. The Office of Management and Budget (OMB) is responsible for reviewing federal agencies' progress in real property management. In 2007, GAO recommended that OMB assist agencies by developing an action plan to address key obstacles associated with decisions related to unneeded real property, including stakeholder influences. In May 2011, the administration proposed legislation, referred to as the Civilian Property Realignment Act (CPRA), to, among other things, establish a legislative framework for disposing of and consolidating civilian real property and that could help limit stakeholder influences in real property decision making.

Chapter 3- The federal real property portfolio, comprising over 900,000 buildings and structures and worth hundreds of billions of dollars, presents management challenges. In January 2003, GAO designated the management of federal real property as a high-risk area in part due to the presence of unneeded property. The Office of Management and Budget (OMB) is responsible for reviewing agencies' progress on federal real property management. The General Services Administration (GSA), often referred to as the federal government's landlord, controls more square feet of buildings than any other civilian federal agency. GSA funds real property acquisition, operation, maintenance, and disposal through the rent it collects from tenant agencies that is deposited into the Federal Buildings Fund (FBF). This testimony discusses (1) the scope and costs of the excess real property held by GSA and other federal agencies; and (2) the challenges GSA and other federal agencies face in disposing of excess and underutilized real property. GAO analyzed GSA data from a centralized real property database, reviewed GSA real property plans and previous GAO reports, and interviewed GSA and OMB officials.

Chapter 4- In January 2003, GAO designated federal real property as a high-risk area because of long-standing problems with excess and underutilized property, deteriorating facilities, unreliable real property data, over-reliance on costly leasing, and security challenges. In January 2009, GAO found that agencies have taken some positive steps to address real property issues but that some of the core problems that led to the designation of this area as high risk persist.

Chapter 5- Many federal agencies hold real property that they do not need, including property that is underutilized or excess. Such properties present significant potential risks to federal agencies because they are costly to maintain and could be put to more cost-beneficial uses or sold to generate revenue for the government. We first designated federal real property management as a high-risk area in January 2003 due to longstanding problems with underutilized and excess property, among other things. After our high-risk designation, President George W. Bush added real property management to the President's Management Agenda and directed that the Federal Real Property Profile (FRPP) be established as a comprehensive database of real property under the control and custody of executive branch agencies, with agencies required to report on their real property assets each year. The President also established a goal of disposing of $15 billion in unneeded real property assets by 2015 to encourage agencies to right-size their portfolios by eliminating unneeded property.

Chapter 6- The mission of the General Services Administration (GSA) is to help federal agencies better serve the public by offering, at best value, superior workplaces, expert solutions, acquisition services, and management policies. GSA consists of the Federal Acquisition Service (FAS), the Public Buildings Service (PBS), and various other business lines dedicated to serving the needs of our customers.

Chapter 7- PBS serves as the Federal Government's builder, developer, lessor, and manager of governmentowned and leased properties. PBS is the largest and most diversified real estate organization in the world.

The PBS Office of Real Property Disposal is responsible for managing the utilization and disposal of Federal excess and surplus real property government-wide.

Surplus Federal properties that are not conveyed to state/local governments and other eligible recipients are sold to the public through a competitive bidding process.

In: Federal Real Property Disposition   ISBN: 978-1-62100-048-8
Editor: Iain D. Haque   © 2012 Nova Science Publishers, Inc.

Chapter 1

REAL PROPERTY DISPOSITION: OVERVIEW AND ISSUES FOR THE 112TH CONGRESS[*]

Garrett Hatch

SUMMARY

Federal executive branch agencies hold an extensive real property portfolio that includes nearly 900,000 buildings and structures, and 41 million acres of land worldwide. These assets have been acquired over a period of decades to help agencies fulfill their diverse missions. The government's portfolio encompasses properties with a range of uses, including barracks, health clinics, warehouses, laboratories, national parks, boat docks, and offices. As agencies' missions change over time, so, too, do their real property needs, thereby rendering some assets less useful or unneeded altogether.

Real property disposition is the process by which federal agencies identify and then transfer, donate, or sell facilities and land they no longer need. Disposition is an important asset management function because the costs of maintaining unneeded properties can be substantial, consuming billions of dollars that might be applied to pressing real property needs, such as acquiring new space and repairing existing facilities, or to other policy issues, such as reducing the national debt.

---

[*] This is an edited, reformatted and augmented version of Congressional Research Service publication R41240, dated January 12, 2011.

Audits of agency real property portfolios have found that the government holds thousands of unneeded properties, and must spend hundreds of millions of dollars annually to maintain them. Agencies have said that their disposal efforts are often hampered by legal and budgetary disincentives, and competing stakeholder interests. In addition, Congress is limited in its capacity to conduct oversight of the disposal process because it lacks access to reliable, comprehensive real property data. The government's inability to efficiently dispose of its unneeded property is a major reason that federal real property management has been identified by the Government Accountability Office (GAO) as a "high-risk" area since 2003.

This report begins with an explanation of the real property disposal process, and then discusses some of the factors that have made disposition inefficient and costly. It then examines real property legislation introduced in the 111th Congress that would have addressed those problems, including the Federal Real Property Disposal Enhancement Act of 2009 (H.R. 2495), S.Amdt. 1042, and the President's FY2011 budget request. The report concludes with policy options for enhancing both the disposal process and congressional oversight of it.

INTRODUCTION

Federal executive branch agencies hold an extensive real property portfolio that includes nearly 900,000 buildings and structures, and 41 million acres of land worldwide.[1] These assets have been acquired over a period of decades to help agencies fulfill their diverse missions. Agencies hold properties with a range of uses, including barracks, health clinics, warehouses, laboratories, national parks, boat docks, and offices. As agencies' missions change over time, so, too, do their real property needs, thereby rendering some assets less useful or unneeded altogether. Healthcare provided by the Department of Veterans Affairs (VA), for example, has shifted in recent decades from predominately hospital-based inpatient care to a greater reliance on clinics and outpatient care, with a resulting change in space needs.[2] Similarly, the Department of Defense (DOD) reduced its force structure by 36% after the cold war ended, and has engaged in several rounds of base realignments and installation closures.[3]

Real property disposition is the process by which federal agencies identify and then transfer, donate, or sell facilities and land they no longer need. Disposition is an important asset management function because the costs of maintaining unneeded properties can be substantial, consuming financial resources that might be applied to pressing real property needs, such as acquiring new space and repairing existing facilities, or towards other pressing policy issues, such as reducing the national debt.

Audits of agency real property portfolios have found that the government holds thousands of unneeded properties, and must spend hundreds of millions of dollars annually to maintain them. Agencies have said that their disposal efforts are often hampered by legal and budgetary disincentives, and competing stakeholder interests. In addition, Congress is limited in its capacity to conduct oversight of the disposal process because it lacks access to reliable, comprehensive, real property data. The government's inability to efficiently dispose of its unneeded property is a major reason that federal real property management has been identified by the Government Accountability Office (GAO) as a "high-risk" area since 2003.

This report begins with an explanation of the real property disposal process, and then discusses some of the factors that have made disposition inefficient and costly. It then examines real property legislation introduced in the 111th Congress that would have addressed those problems and concludes with policy options for enhancing both the disposal process and congressional oversight of it.

OVERVIEW OF THE DISPOSITION PROCESS

The Federal Real Property and Administrative Services Act of 1949 (Property Act) applies to real property held by most federal agencies.[4] The Property Act authorizes the General Services Administration (GSA) to dispose of real property that agencies no longer need, although some agencies have been granted the authority to dispose of their own property.[5] Agencies without independent disposal authority generally follow the process described in this section.

Federal Transfer

In order to identify properties that agencies no longer need, each agency is required to conduct an annual survey of its real property holdings. Properties that are no longer needed are reported to GSA as "excess."[6] GSA then physically inspects each excess property, and hires a licensed appraiser to evaluate its fair market value.[7] Next, GSA sends a written Notice of Availability describing the property to other federal agencies, and posts information about the property on its Property Disposal Resource Center website.[8] Agencies may also identify unneeded assets available for transfer through the Federal Real Property Profile (FRPP), a database of the buildings, structures, and land held by federal agencies.[9] If an agency wants to acquire an excess property, it must respond to the Notice of Availability within 30 days, and then submit a formal request for the property to be transferred within 60 days from the date the notice expires. Agencies are required to pay fair market value to acquire excess property, although there are a number of circumstances under which an exception to this requirement may be approved.[10]

Public Benefit Conveyance

If no federal agency wants an unneeded property, then it is declared "surplus," and it is made available to state and local governments, and non-profits.[11] These entities may have surplus property transferred to them for a discount of up to 100% of fair market value, provided they use the property for a public benefit.[12] This type of transfer is called a public benefit conveyance, and to qualify, the property must be used for one of the following purposes (not listed in order of preference):

- Homeless services
- Corrections
- Law enforcement
- Public health
- Drug rehabilitation
- Education
- Parks and recreation
- Seaport facilities
- Wildlife conservation
- Highways
- Emergency Management Response
- Historic monuments
- Public airports
- Housing

Each public benefit category has a federal agency, called a sponsor, that oversees conveyances for that purpose. Generally, sponsoring agencies have expertise in the policy areas they sponsor. The Federal Aviation Administration, for example, is the sponsoring agency for public airport conveyances.[13]

Pursuant to Title V of the McKinney-Vento Homeless Assistance Act, surplus properties must be made available for serving the homeless before being made available for other public benefit uses.[14] The Department of Housing and Urban Development (HUD) is responsible for reviewing surplus property to determine if it is suitable for homeless use. If a property is determined to be unsuitable for homeless use, then it becomes available for other public uses at that time. If HUD determines a surplus property is suitable, however, it publishes a notice to that effect in the *Federal Register*. State and local governments, and non-profits, are given 60 days to notify the sponsoring agency, the Department of Health and Human Services (HHS), that they are interested in using the property for serving the homeless.[15] If HHS receives an expression of interest within the 60-day window, the property may not be made available for any other purpose until action on the request is complete. If no interest is expressed, then the property becomes available for other public benefit uses.[16] GSA advertises its availability by contacting state and local officials, and known non-profits with an interest in the property. GSA may also post notices in city halls, state capitols, and other appropriate locations.[17] The sponsoring agency is generally responsible for distributing, reviewing, and approving applications; conveying the property to the recipient; and monitoring the use of the property after it has been transferred, although GSA assists some agencies with these duties.[18] If the recipient of a conveyed property fails to use the property as agreed—by building a retail center on property conveyed for a public park, for example—then the property may revert back to the federal government.

Negotiated Sale

Surplus property that is not disposed of through the public benefit conveyance process may be sold to state and local governments at fair market value.[19] In essence, state and local governments are given the right of first refusal—they are allowed an opportunity to purchase surplus property before the property is offered for sale to the general public. Federal real property regulations permit negotiated sales when "a public benefit, which would not be realized from a competitive sale, will result from the negotiated sale."[20] The regulations do not specify what types of activities would qualify, but GSA guidance notes that a state or local government can use property "according to its own redevelopment needs," including economic development.[21]

Public Sale

Surplus properties that are still available after screening for public benefit conveyance and negotiated sale may be offered for public sale. The property is advertised in local newspapers, regional or national publications, and the U.S. Real Estate Sales list, and may also be found on GSA's website.[22] The appraised value of a property is used as a guideline for initial pricing, and properties are sold through sealed bids, physical auctions, and Internet auctions.[23]

OBSTACLES TO EFFICIENT DISPOSITION

According to GAO, weaknesses in the disposition process have left the government with a large inventory of unneeded properties.[24] The most recent comprehensive data available showed that the government held nearly 22,000 excess and surplus properties in 2007.[25] While government-wide data are not available on the cost of maintaining unneeded properties, audits have shown these costs to be a substantial expense for some agencies. GAO auditors estimated, for example, that the VA spent $175 million on operating and maintaining unneeded facilities in 2007,[26] and that DOD spent between $3 billion and $4 billion dollars in 2003 to maintain facilities that were not needed.[27] Agencies have said that the financial and administrative burdens associated with disposition have hindered their efforts to transfer, convey, and sell their unneeded properties, and that competing stakeholder interests may delay or halt disposal of some properties altogether. In addition, the quality of data available to real property managers for strategic decision making has been called into question. Each of these issues is discussed below.

Budgetary Disincentives

Federal agencies frequently cite the cost of complying with environmental regulations as a major disincentive to disposal. Generally speaking, agencies are required to assess and pay for any environmental cleanup that may be needed before disposing of a property. Identifying and addressing environmental hazards, such as lead paint, asbestos, medical waste, and soil contamination, prior to disposition can result in "significant" up-front costs for agencies.[28] Some agencies must complete expensive repairs and renovations before disposing of certain properties, like repairs to meet health and safety standards, or to restore historic sites in accordance with federal standards. VA, for example, estimated that it would need to spend about $3 billion to repair the buildings in its portfolio that it rated in "poor" or "critical" condition— 56% of which were vacant or underutilized, and therefore would be candidates for disposal.[29] Agencies that wish to demolish vacant buildings and structures face deconstruction and cleanup costs that, at times, exceed the cost of maintaining the property—at least in the short run—which may encourage real property managers to retain the property rather than dispose of it.[30]

These problems are compounded by the fact that, historically, agencies have not been able to recoup the costs of disposition by retaining the proceeds resulting from the sale of a property. In recent years, some agencies have been granted the authority to retain net proceeds, to varying degrees.[31] There is wide support for this policy among agency real property officials: GAO interviewed officials at the 10 largest landholding agencies and found that nearly all of the officials that had the authority considered it to be "a strong incentive to sell real property," and those that did not have that authority wanted it.[32]

Administrative Burden

Agencies have also argued that disposal regulations create an administrative burden that delays disposition and drives up costs even further. Some agencies have noted that the need to screen properties for homeless use, as required by the McKinney-Vento Act, slows down the disposition process unnecessarily in some cases. The Department of Energy, for example, told auditors that they had properties that they felt could be disposed of only by demolition, due to their condition or location, but that still had to go through the homeless screening process. VA officials have said the requirements of the McKinney-Vento Act can add as much as two years to the disposal process, during which time maintenance costs continue to be incurred.[33] Similarly, it may take agencies years of study to assess the potential environmental consequences of a proposed disposal, and to develop and implement an abatement plan.[34] Agencies also say it takes longer to dispose of historic properties, because the National Historic Preservation Act requires them to plan their disposal actions so as to minimize the harm they cause to the historic property, which may include time-consuming procedures such as consulting with historic preservation groups at the state, local, and federal level.[35]

Stakeholder Conflict

Some agencies have found their disposal efforts complicated by the involvement of stakeholders with competing agendas. In 2002, for example, the United States Postal Service (USPS) identified a number of "redundant, low-value" facilities that it sought to close in order to reduce its operating costs.[36] As part of the facility closure process, USPS was required to formally announce its intention to close each facility and solicit comments from the community.[37] USPS ultimately abandoned its plans to close many facilities it identified—including post offices that were underutilized, in poor condition, or not critical to serving their geographic areas—in part due to political pressure from stakeholders.[38] The Department of the Interior has said that it can be stymied by the competing concerns of local and state governments, historic preservation offices, and other political factors, when attempting to dispose of some of its unneeded real property.[39] Similarly, VA has found that communities sometimes oppose disposals that would result in new development, and veterans groups have opposed disposing of building space if that space would be used for purposes unrelated to the needs of veterans.[40] The Department of State has had difficulty in disposing of surplus real property overseas, due to disputes with host governments that restrict property sales.[41] These conflicts can result in delay, or even cancellation of proposed disposals, which, in turn, prevents agencies from reducing their expenditures on unneeded properties.

CONCERNS WITH REAL PROPERTY DATA

The Federal Real Property Profile (FRPP) is the government's most comprehensive source of information about real property under the control of executive branch agencies. GSA manages the FRPP and is authorized to collect real property data from 24 of the largest landholding agencies each year (other agencies are encouraged, but not required, to report data to GSA).[42] The data elements that participating agencies collect and report are determined by the Federal Real Property Council (FRPC), an interagency taskforce which is funded and chaired by the Office of Management and Budget (OMB). The other members of the council are agency Senior Real Property Officers (SRPOs) and GSA.

The FRPP contains data that could enhance congressional oversight of federal real property activities, such as the number of excess and surplus properties held by major landholding agencies, the annual costs of maintaining those properties, and agency disposition actions. GSA, however, maintains tight control over access to the FRPP, and does not permit direct access to the public and most federal employees, including congressional staff. GSA does consider requests for real property data from congressional offices, but GSA staff query the database and provide the results to the requestor.

Some FRPP data are made public through an annual summary report posted on GSA's website, but the summary reports are of limited use for several reasons.[43] Most of the data are highly aggregated (e.g., the number of assets disposed through public benefit conveyance government-wide), and very limited information is provided on an agency-by-agency basis. It is not possible, therefore, for Congress to monitor the performance of individual agencies through the summary reports. Basic questions, such as how many excess properties each agency disposed of in a given fiscal year, and by what method, cannot be answered. Nor is it possible to compare the performance of agencies, which in turn limits the ability of Congress to study the policies and practices at the most successful agencies and hold poorly performing agencies accountable.

Also, the quality of the FRPP data has been questioned. GAO audits have found, for example, that certain real property data were incomplete or were not comparable across agencies, which limited the usefulness of those data for decision making.[44] In addition, the reports may miscategorize important data on disposal methods. The two most recently published FRPPs identify "other" as the most common disposition method, accounting for 46% (16,028) of the total number of real property assets disposed by agencies in FY2007 and nearly 73% (17,939) of those disposed in FY2008.[45] Typically, the "other" data category is reserved for a relatively small number of cases that do not clearly fit into one of the major data categories, so it is unusual to see such a large number of "other" dispositions. In fact, the FRPP defines "other" disposals as those "that cannot be classified in any of the other disposition methods," so the relatively large percentage of "other" dispositions may reflect misreporting by agencies.[46] If so, then the data reported for all types of dispositions may be of little use, because thousands of properties may have been miscategorized.

The summary reports also omit data that Congress might find valuable. The FRPP contains, for example, the number of excess properties held by each agency and the annual operating costs of those properties—issues about which Congress has expressed ongoing interest—but the summary report only provides the number and annual operating costs of disposed assets, thereby providing the "good news" of future costs avoided through disposition while omitting the "bad news" of the ongoing operating costs associated with unneeded properties the government maintained. Similarly, agencies estimate a dollar amount for the repair needs of their buildings and structures as part of their FRPP reporting, but the estimate is then folded into a formula for calculating a "condition index" for each building.[47] Given that repair needs are an obstacle to disposing of some properties, Congress may find it useful to have the repair estimates reported separately to help inform funding decisions.

SELECT REAL PROPERTY PROPOSALS

H.R. 2495

Congress has shown an ongoing interest in real property disposal reform, and in the 111th Congress, Representative Dennis Moore introduced H.R. 2495, the Federal Real Property Disposal Enhancement Act of 2009.[48] Among the major provisions of the bill, GSA would have been required to submit an annual report to Congress that included information on the number, market value, and deferred maintenance costs of all executive branch real property assets.[49] For surplus properties, the report would have also included ongoing maintenance costs, and, for surplus properties that had been disposed of, the report would have provided the size, location, market value, and method of disposal used. All of the data would have been "set forth government-wide, and by agency, and for each at the constructed asset level and at the facility/installation level." This would have required reporting for individual buildings, parcels of land, and structures.

H.R. 2495 would have provided new financial resources for agency disposal activities. The bill would have allowed agencies to retain the net proceeds from the disposition of real property, and to use those funds, as authorized by Congress, for real property activities, including the maintenance, repair, and disposal of other properties.[50] The bill would also have given GSA the authority to pay for the costs of preparing properties held by other agencies for disposal, and then required agencies to reimburse GSA from the proceeds of the sale of the property.

In addition, the bill would have established a demonstration program that would exempt certain properties from the McKinney-Vento Act—primarily buildings and structures that, due to their condition or location, would not likely be approved for homeless use—so that they may be demolished without being delayed by the act's homeless screening requirements.

Other provisions in H.R. 2495 would have required GSA to issue recommendations to executive agencies on how to identify excess property, how to evaluate the costs and benefits of disposition, how to prioritize disposal decisions, and how to best dispose of excess property. Executive agencies, for their part, would have been required to ensure that they were identifying, reporting, and disposing of excess property as promptly as possible. Agencies would have been further required to establish "goals and incentives" for reducing excess real property in their inventories.

S.Amdt. 1042

On May 5, 2009, Senator Tom Coburn introduced S.Amdt. 1042, which would have established a pilot program to expedite disposition of unneeded properties.[51] The amendment, which was ruled out of order, would have applied to all landholding agencies, and the pilot program would have terminated five years after the amendment was enacted. The amendment would have required the Director of OMB to select properties for the pilot program that were deemed excess, surplus, "underperforming," or "otherwise not meeting the needs" of the government, as defined by the Director.[52] Information about the selected properties—including their suitability for homeless use—would have been posted on a publicly accessible website. The Secretary of Housing and Urban Development would have been required to review the properties selected for the pilot program by the OMB Director, and determine whether each one was suitable for homeless use. If a property was determined to be suitable for homeless use, it would have been made available to state and local government agencies, and non-profit organizations that provide services to the homeless. If a property was determined to be unsuitable for homeless use, or if the property was deemed suitable but it was not conveyed to a homeless serving entity, then it would have been eligible for expedited disposition. The expedited disposal process would have permitted agencies to demolish or sell properties at fair market value without first requiring those properties to be offered for public benefit conveyance (beyond homeless use screening, which they would have already completed). In addition, agencies would have been permitted to retain 20% of the net proceeds from the disposal of their properties (the remaining 80% would have been deposited into the Treasury as miscellaneous receipts), and those funds would have been available for real property capital improvements, such as repairs and renovations, as well as other disposal activities. The amendment would have required GAO to study the pilot program within three years of enactment and to report the results to Congress.

President Obama's FY2011 Budget Request

The Administrations of Presidents George W. Bush and Barack Obama have both proposed real property disposal initiatives as part of their budget submissions. President Obama's FY2011 budget request included proposed language that was similar to the language in H.R. 2495 in several respects, including language that would require GSA to submit an annual real property report to Congress.[53] The real property report that the President proposed would have included data on the number and value of all real property held by federal agencies, reported government-wide, by agency, and at the facility or installation level. Deferred maintenance costs for agency real property would also have been reported at the government-wide and agency levels, but not by facility or installation. The report would have included data on the number, value, and ongoing maintenance costs associated with excess properties, reported government-wide and by agency. Data on surplus real property that is disposed of would also have been included in the report, including data on each property's location, size, value, and method of disposal used. For surplus properties demolished or disposed of through a public benefit conveyance, the report would have included an estimate of the net savings to the government that resulted from the disposal. It is not clear whether "value" referred to the estimated market value of a property, or its replacement value.

The President also proposed establishing a public website at GSA that would provide some data on federal real property holdings. At a minimum, the website would have provided the location, size, status (e.g., excess or surplus), and "mission criticality" of each property. The latter term appears to have been related to the "mission dependency" data GSA currently collects for the FRPP. A property is deemed mission critical, according to the FRPP data dictionary, if an agency's mission would be compromised without a particular constructed asset or parcel of land.[54] Properties may also be rated "mission dependent, but not critical" and "not mission dependent" in the FRPP. The proposal specifies that GSA may withhold information from the website if doing so would be in the best interest of the government or the public, or for national security reasons.

In addition, the President's proposal would have permitted agencies to retain net proceeds from the disposal of real property, and to use those funds, as authorized by Congress, for real property activities, including the maintenance, repair, and disposal of other properties.[55] The President's proposal would also have required, in a manner similar to the requirements of H.R. 2495, that executive agencies ensure that they were identifying, reporting, and disposing of excess property as promptly as possible, and that they establish "goals and incentives" for reducing excess real property in their inventories.

The budget request would also have established a real property disposal pilot program. The President's proposal would have permitted agencies to recommend for the pilot program any "real property that is not meeting Federal Government needs," although the Director of OMB would have determined both the criteria for participation in the program and which properties were selected. The proposal would have attempted to expedite disposal by permitting properties to be offered for sale without being screened for public benefit conveyance, including homeless use. Properties sold under the pilot program must not obtain less than fair market value.

While President Obama may have needed legislation to establish the pilot program and to enable agencies to retain net proceeds, it appears other elements of his real property proposal might not have required congressional approval. The annual report and the public website, for instance, could have been implemented through executive action.

CONCLUDING OBSERVATIONS

The three proposals discussed in the previous section—H.R. 2495, S.Amdt. 1042, and the President's budget request—vary in their scope, authorities, and requirements, and so would have different consequences if enacted. Table 1, below, outlines how each proposal would have addressed the four obstacles to efficient real property disposition discussed in this report: budgetary disincentives, administrative burden, stakeholder conflict, and lack of access to comprehensive, accurate data.

**Table 1. How Select Legislative Proposals
Address Obstacles to Efficient Disposition**

	H.R. 2495	S.Amdt. 1042	FY2011 Budget
Budgetary Disincentives	Agencies retain all of net proceeds from disposal	Agencies retain 20% of net proceeds from disposal	Agencies retain all of net proceeds from disposal
Administrative Burden	Properties in expedited demolition pilot program exempt from homeless use screening	Properties in expedited disposal pilot program exempt from most PBC screening requirements	Properties in expedited sale pilot program exempt from all PBC screening requirements
Stakeholder Conflict	Does not address	Does not address	Does not address
Data Concerns	Detailed data on all agency real property required in annual report	Basic data on pilot program properties posted online	Basic data on all agency real property posted online; detailed data reported annually

Note: PBC refers to Public Benefit Conveyance.

H.R. 2495 would have potentially enhanced the ability of agencies to dispose of unneeded properties by permitting them to retain the net proceeds from dispositions. It is not clear how much of an effect this provision would have had, however, because H.R. 2495 would have permitted agencies to use net proceeds for a range of real property activities—not just for the disposal of unneeded properties. An agency could have chosen, for example, to apply some or all of its net proceeds towards repairs at buildings the agency intends to continue to utilize, which would reduce the amount of funds available for disposition activities. Given that agency repair needs are in the billions, and net proceeds in FY2008 were $134 million, the former could consume a large share of the latter, depending on agency priorities.[56] The pilot program established by H.R. 2495 would have potentially reduced the time it takes to dispose of one category of unneeded real property—buildings and structures scheduled for demolition—but it would not have included unneeded properties that would be disposed of by transfer, sale, or public benefit conveyance. In addition, the number of properties demolished under the pilot program may have been limited by the extent to which the cost of environmental cleanup acts as a disincentive. The annual report required by H.R. 2495 would have addressed many of the concerns about the current lack of comprehensive real property data, and it would provide useful information about properties the government no longer needs, including disposal actions. It is possible that GSA might have objected to the inclusion of each property's estimated market value in the report, as it considers market information to be confidential.

Unlike H.R. 2495 and the President's budget request, S.Amdt. 1042 would have permitted agencies to retain 20%, rather than all, of net proceeds. Using FY2008 net proceeds data, the amendment would have provided $27 million for agency real property activities, government-wide, about $107 million less than H.R. 2495 and the President's proposal would have provided. The amendment's expedited disposal program would have potentially reduced the administrative burden associated with disposing of most unneeded properties by exempting them from all public benefit conveyance requirements, other than screening for homeless use. State and local governments and non-profits might object to the pilot program, because by "skipping" most of the PBC process it would have reduced the number of federal properties they may obtain at a discount. On the other hand, state and local governments, and private firms, might support this type of pilot program because it would have increased the number of federal properties that could be purchased—and therefore be used for a wider range of purposes, including economic development, than if the property had been conveyed. The amendment would have required a limited set of data to be made available to the public, primarily information pertaining to the suitability of each property in the pilot program for homeless use.

If enacted, the President's real property proposal would have provided access to all net disposal proceeds as a source of real property funding, although the effect of that funding on disposition cannot easily be estimated, because the proposal, like H.R. 2495, would not have limited the use of net proceeds to disposal activities. The President's proposal would have reduced the administrative burden for all properties in the pilot program by exempting them from public benefit conveyance requirements, including homeless use. Opposition to the pilot program may have been found among some state and local government agencies, and non-profit organizations that prefer to have access to surplus federal property through public conveyance, and particularly among those agencies and non-profits that serve the homeless, because they had been given special consideration under McKinney-Vento. These exemptions could have cut months from the disposal process for many properties, however, thereby reducing maintenance costs and providing the government with the opportunity to realize revenues from the sale of properties sooner. The database proposed in the President's budget would have had a broad scope—encompassing nearly all agency real property—but the data would have been primarily limited to descriptive information. In addition, agencies might have objected to having the mission criticality of their properties included in the database. It could be argued that identifying mission critical facilities on a public website, and providing the addresses of those facilities, is not in the interest of national security. The annual real property report proposed by the President's would have addressed the need for increased data on agency excess and surplus properties and disposal actions, although it would not appear to have provided data on the cost of maintaining unneeded properties at the individual asset level (building, structure, or parcel of land).

None of the three proposals addressed stakeholder conflict. GAO has argued that stakeholder conflict might be reduced if agencies had an "independent apparatus" for making real property disposal decisions.[57] GAO also suggested that the process by which the Department of Defense disposes of property under the Base Realignment Closure Act (BRAC) might serve as a model for civilian agencies seeking to diminish the effect of competing stakeholder interests, but it did not elaborate.[58]

Enhanced Use Leases

It may not be possible for agencies to sell some unneeded properties, particularly when the real estate market is slow. Congress may therefore wish to consider whether to expand the authority of agencies to enter into Enhanced Use Leases (EULs). In broad terms, EULs are special authorities that permit agencies to enter into short- or long-term lease agreements with public and private entities for the use of federal property. VA has an EUL in New Jersey, for example, that has turned an underutilized property into an industrial park, and it leases unneeded space in Los Angeles on a short-term basis to the film industry.[59] Because EULs are typically provided to individual agencies, the scope of the authority they grant varies widely. Many agencies can retain the proceeds generated by EULs, for example, but others cannot.[60] Similarly, some agencies may use EUL proceeds for activities unrelated to real property, while others may apply them only to real property functions.[61] While EULs may provide revenue to agencies they may not otherwise realize, some agencies find the process of drafting, negotiating, and implementing an EUL agreement to be time consuming and complicated.[62] If Congress does consider expanding EUL authorities, among the issues it might choose to examine are whether to require congressional approval before EUL proceeds may be used by an agency, and whether to limit the use of proceeds to certain purposes (e.g., only disposal, any real property activity, any agency activity).

End Notes

[1] These figures do not include real property owned by the federal judicial or legislative branches. Federal Real Property Council, *FY2008 Federal Real Property Report: An Overview of the U.S. Federal Government's Real Property Assets*, August 2009, p. 9.

[2] U.S. Government Accountability Office, *Federal Real Property: Progress Made in Reducing Unneeded Property, but VA Needs Better Information to Make Further Reductions*, GAO-08-939, September 2008, p. 9.

[3] U.S. Government Accountability Office, *Federal Real Property: Excess and Underutilized Property is an Ongoing Problem*, GAO-06-248, February 2006, p. 3. For more information, see CRS Report R40476, *Base Realignment and Closure (BRAC): Transfer and Disposal of Military Property*, by R. Chuck Mason.

[4] 40 U.S.C. § 101 et. seq. Land reserved for national forest or national park purposes, and Bureau of Land Management properties, are not covered by these disposal rules. Other legislation that governs federal agency real property disposal includes the National Historic Preservation Act (16 U.S.C. § 470 et. seq.), which establishes guidelines for agency disposition of historic properties, and the Stewart B. McKinney Homeless Assistance Act (42 U.S.C. § 11411), which requires agencies to make surplus real property available first for homeless use before making it available for other purposes. In addition, Executive Order 13327, signed in 2004 by President George W. Bush, established (1) Senior Real Property Officers (SRPOs) at 24 of the largest landholding agencies to monitor and manage their agencies' real property, (2) a Federal Real Property Council, comprised of SRPOs, to evaluate agency real property policies and practices, and (3) the Federal Real Property Profile, a database with information on agency real property holdings, including disposition data.

[5] The Department of Defense has the authority to dispose of unneeded real property that is subject to the Base Realignment and Closure (BRAC) process, but GSA disposes of non-BRAC real property. The United States Postal Service has the authority to dispose of all of its real property. The Departments of State, Veterans Affairs, Education, Health and Human Services, the Interior, and Agriculture also have the authority to dispose of some unneeded real property, although the scope of that authority varies widely.

[6] 40 U.S.C. § 102.

[7] U.S. General Services Administration, *Customer Guide to Real Property Disposal*, p. 17, at http://www.missionumatilla.com/documents/historical_data/HD0013_PropertyDisposalClosureGuide_GSA

[8] The Office of Real Property Utilization and Disposal website address is https://extportal.pbs.gsa.gov/ResourceCenter/ viewproperties.do?noticetype=1.

[9] Only the 24 federal agencies are required to report their real property data annually to the FRPP, although other agencies have the option of reporting. The agencies that are required

to report are the Departments of Agriculture, Commerce, Defense, Education, Energy, Health and Human Services, Homeland Security, Housing and Urban Development, the Interior, Justice, Labor, State, Transportation, the Treasury, and Veterans Affairs; Environmental Protection Agency; General Services Administration; National Aeronautics and Space Administration; National Science Foundation; Nuclear Regulatory Commission; Office of Personnel Management; Small Business Administration; Social Security Administration; and United States Agency for International Development.

[10] See 41 CFR § 102-75.1275; 41 CFR §§ 102-75.190-102-75.225; and 40 U.S.C. § 522. When an agency is required to pay fair market value for a property, the government does not realize any new revenue since the funds are being transferred from another federal agency.

[11] 40 U.S.C. § 102.

[12] 40 U.S.C. § 549.

[13] 40 U.S.C. § 550. The agencies that sponsor conveyances are the Departments of Education (education), Health and Human Services (public health, homeless services), the Interior (parks and recreation, historic monuments, wildlife conservation), Justice (correctional), Transportation (port facility), Housing and Urban Development (housing), Justice (law enforcement), Homeland Security (emergency management response), and the Federal Aviation Authority (public airports).

[14] 42 U.S.C. 11411.

[15] 41 CFR § 102-75.1200.

[16] Conveyances, other than McKinney Act transfers, are at the discretion of the agency and are not required by statute.

[17] U.S. General Services Administration, *Surplus Real Property Available for Public Use: Notification Procedure*, GSA website, at
http://www.gsa.gov/Portal/gsa/ep/contentView.do?contentType=GSA

[18] U.S. General Services Administration, *Customer Guide to Real Property*, p. 25. The General Services Administration is responsible for deeding, conveyance, and compliance monitoring of correctional, law enforcement, and emergency management conveyances, and for just deeding and conveyance of properties to be used for historic monuments, or public airports.

[19] 41 CFR § 102-75.880(d); 40 U.S.C. § 545.

[20] Ibid.

[21] U.S. General Services Administration, Office of Real Property Utilization and Disposal, "How to Acquire Federal Property," at
https://extportal.pbs.gsa.gov/ResourceCenter/content/acquireFedProp.do.

[22] General Services Administration, Office of Real Property Utilization and Disposal, Current Sales webpage, at
https://extportal.pbs.gsa.gov/ResourceCenter/PRHomePage/loadPRHomePage.do?type=full

[23] General Services Administration, *Customer Guide to Real Property Disposal*, p. 27.

[24] U.S. Government Accountability Office, *High-Risk Series: Federal Real Property*, GAO-03-122, January 2003, p. 4.

[25] Office of Management and Budget, *Response to Section 408 of P.L. 109-396*, June 15, 2007, p. 2. GSA publishes an annual real property report, but that report does not identify the number of excess and surplus properties held by federal agencies.

[26] U.S. Government Accountability Office, *Federal Real Property: Progress Made in Reducing Unneeded Property, but VA needs Better Information to Make Further Reductions*, GAO-08-939, September 2008, p. 4.

[27] U.S Government Accountability Office, *Federal Real Property: Excess and Underutilized Property Is an Ongoing Problem*, GAO-06-258, February 2006, p. 6.

[28] U.S. Government Accountability Office, *Federal Real Property: Progress Made Toward Addressing Problems, but Underlying Obstacles Continue to Hamper Reform*, GAO-07-349, April 13, 2007, p. 40.

[29] U.S. Government Accountability Office, *Federal Real Property: Progress Made in Reducing Unneeded Property, but VA needs Better Information to Make Further Reductions*, GAO-08-939, September 2008, p. 5.

[30] U.S. Government Accountability Office, *Federal Real Property: Progress Made Toward Addressing Problems, but Underlying Obstacles Continue to Hamper Reform*, GAO-07-349, April 13, 2007, pp. 40-41.

[31] U.S. Government Accountability Office, *Federal Real Property: An Update on High-Risk Issues*, GAO-09-801, July 15, 2009, p. 18.

[32] Ibid., p. 19.

[33] U.S. Government Accountability Office, *Federal Real Property: Progress Made in Reducing Unneeded Property, but VA needs Better Information to Make Further Reductions*, GAO-08-939, September 2008, p. 39.

[34] U.S. Government Accountability Office, *High-Risk Series: Federal Real Property*, GAO-03-122, January 2003, p. 41.

[35] U.S. Government Accountability Office, *Federal Real Property: DHS Has Made Progress, but Additional Actions Are Needed to Address Real Property Management and Security Challenges*, GAO-07-658, June 2007, p. 42.

[36] U.S. Government Accountability Office, *U.S. Postal Service Facilities: Improvements in Data Would Strengthen Maintenance and Alignment of Access to Retail Services*, December 2007, GAO-08-41 p. 39.

[37] Ibid.

[38] U.S. Government Accountability Office, *Federal Real Property: An Update on High-Risk Issues*, GAO-09-801, July 15, 2009, p. 15.

[39] Ibid., p. 16.

[40] U.S. Government Accountability Office, *Federal Real Property: Progress Made in Reducing Unneeded Property, but VA needs Better Information to Make Further Reductions*, GAO-08-939, September 2008, p. 5.

[41] U.S. Government Accountability Office, *High-Risk Series: Federal Real Property*, GAO-03-122, January 2003, p. 40.

[42] Executive Order 13327, "Federal Real Property Asset Management," 69 *Federal Register* 5897, February 4, 2004. According to the provisions of E.O. 13327, only the 24 agencies listed in 31 U.S.C. 901(b)(1) and (b)(2) are required to report real property data to GSA. Those agencies are the Departments of Agriculture, Commerce, Defense, Education, Energy, Health and Human Services, Homeland Security, Housing and Urban Development, the Interior, Justice, Labor, State, Transportation, the Treasury, and Veterans Affairs; Environmental Protection Agency; General Services Administration; National Aeronautics and Space Administration; National Science Foundation; Nuclear Regulatory Commission; Office of Personnel Management; Small Business Administration; Social Security Administration; and United States Agency for International Development.

[43] The annual real property summary reports may be found on GSA's Federal Real Property Report Library website, at
http://www.gsa.gov/Portal/gsa/ep/contentView.do?contentType=GSA

[44] U.S. Government Accountability Office, *Federal Real Property: An Update on High-Risk Issues*, GAO-09-801, July 15, 2009, p. 10.

[45] Federal Real Property Council, *FY2008 Federal Real Property Report: An Overview of the U.S. Federal Government's Real Property Assets*, August 2009, p. 24.

[46] Ibid.

[47] U.S. General Services Administration, Office of Governmentwide Policy, *FY2008 Federal Real Property Report*, August 2009, p. 30.

[48] H.R. 2495 was introduced May 19, 2009. Representatives Duncan, Boyd, and Hill cosponsored the bill. It was ordered to be reported by the House Oversight and Government Reform Committee on September 10, 2009. No further action on the bill has been taken.

[49] Deferred maintenance costs are generally considered to be the cost of repairs needed to bring a property to current standards.

[50] The bill specifies that net proceeds from the sale of reverted property that had been conveyed for a public benefit would be deposited into GSA's real property account.

[51] *Congressional Record*, vol. 156, no. 68 (May 5, 2009), S5164-S5166. Senator Coburn's amendment would have amended S.Amdt. 1040, which in turn proposed to amend S. 896, the Helping Families Save Their Homes Act of 2009 (P.L. 111-22).

[52] The amendment did not define either the term "underperforming" or the phrase "not meeting the needs of the Federal Government."

[53] The White House, Office of Management and Budget, *Budget of the United States for Fiscal Year 2011, Appendix*, p. 16-17 (Washington: GPO, 2010).

[54] Federal Real Property Council, *2009 Guidance for Real Property Inventory Reporting*, July 14, 2009, p. 11, at
http://www.gsa.gov/graphics/ogp/2009_Guidance_for_Real_Property_Inventory_Reporting.pdf.

[55] As with the language in H.R. 2495, the President's proposal specifies that net proceeds from the sale of reverted property that had been conveyed for a public benefit would be deposited into GSA's real property account.

[56] Federal Real Property Council, *FY2008 Federal Real Property Report: An Overview of the U.S. Federal Government's Real Property Assets*, August 2009, p. 24.

[57] Government Accountability Office, *Federal Real Property: Excess and Underutilized Property is an Ongoing Problem*, GAO-06-248, February 2006, p. 10.

[58] Government Accountability Office, *Federal Real Property: An Update on High Risk Issues*, GAO-09-801, July 2009, p. 16.

[59] Government Accountability Office, *VA Real Property: VA Emphasizes Enhanced-Use Leases to Manage Its Real Property Portfolio*, GAO-09-776, June 2009, p. 3.

[60] Government Accountability Office, *Federal Real Property: Authorities and Actions Regarding Enhanced Use Leases and Sale of Unneeded Real Property*, GAO-09-283, February 17, 2009, p. 5.

[61] Ibid., pp. 14-15.

[62] Government Accountability Office, *VA Real Property: VA Emphasizes Enhanced-Use Leases to Manage Its Real Property Portfolio*, GAO-09-776, June 2009, pp. 5-6.

In: Federal Real Property Disposition   ISBN: 978-1-62100-048-8
Editor: Iain D. Haque   © 2012 Nova Science Publishers, Inc.

Chapter 2

FEDERAL REAL PROPERTY: PROPOSED CIVILIAN BOARD COULD ADDRESS DISPOSAL OF UNNEEDED FACILITIES[*]

United States Government Accountability Office

WHY GAO DID THIS STUDY

The federal government holds more than 45,000 underutilized properties that cost nearly $1.7 billion annually to operate, yet significant obstacles impede efforts to close, consolidate, or find other uses for these properties. GAO has designated federal real property management as a high-risk area, in part because of the number and cost of these properties. The Office of Management and Budget (OMB) is responsible for reviewing federal agencies' progress in real property management. In 2007, GAO recommended that OMB assist agencies by developing an action plan to address key obstacles associated with decisions related to unneeded real property, including stakeholder influences. In May 2011, the administration proposed legislation, referred to as the Civilian Property Realignment Act (CPRA), to, among other things, establish a legislative framework for disposing of and consolidating civilian real property and that could help limit stakeholder influences in real property decision making.

---

[*] This is an edited, reformatted and augmented version of the United States Government Accountability Office publication, GAO-11-704T, dated June 9, 2011.

This statement identifies (1) progress the government has made toward addressing obstacles to federal real property management, (2) some of the challenges that remain and how CPRA may be responsive to those challenges, and (3) key elements of the Department of Defense's (DOD) base realignment and closure (BRAC) process that could expedite the disposal of unneeded civilian properties. To do this work, GAO relied on its prior work, and reviewed CPRA and other relevant reports.

WHAT GAO FOUND

In designating federal real property management as a high-risk area, GAO reported that despite the magnitude and complexity of real-property-related problems, there was no governmentwide strategic focus on real property issues and governmentwide data were unreliable and outdated. The administration and real-property-holding agencies have subsequently improved their strategic management of real property by establishing an interagency Federal Real Property Council designed to enhance real property planning processes and implementing controls to improve the reliability of federal real property data.

Even with this progress, problems related to unneeded property and leasing persist because the government has not yet addressed other challenges to effective real property management, such as legal and financial limitations and stakeholder influences. CPRA is somewhat responsive to these challenges. For example, CPRA proposes an independent board that would streamline the disposal process by selecting properties it considers appropriate for public benefit uses. This streamlined process could reduce disposal time and costs. CPRA would also establish an Asset Proceeds and Space Management Fund that could be used to reimburse agencies for necessary disposal costs. The proposed independent board would address stakeholder influences by recommending federal properties for disposal or consolidation after receiving recommendations from civilian landholding agencies and independently reviewing the agencies' recommendations. CPRA does not explicitly address the government's overreliance on leasing, but could help do so through board recommendations for consolidating operations where appropriate. GAO is currently examining issues related to leasing costs and excess property.

Certain key elements of DOD's BRAC process—which, like CPRA, was designed to address obstacles to closures or realignments—may be applicable to the disposal and realignment of real property governmentwide. These elements include establishing goals, developing criteria for evaluating closures and realignments, estimating the costs and savings anticipated from implementing recommendations, and involving the audit community. A key similarity between BRAC and CPRA is that both establish an independent board to review agency recommendations. A key difference is that while the BRAC process places the Secretary of Defense in a central role to review and submit candidate recommendations to the independent board, CPRA does not provide for any similar central role for civilian agencies.

STATEMENT OF DAVID J. WISE,
DIRECTOR, PHYSICAL INFRASTRUCTURE ISSUES
BRIAN J. LEPORE, DIRECTOR,
DEFENSE CAPABILITIES AND MANAGEMENT ISSUES

Chairman Carper, Ranking Member Brown, and Members of the Subcommittee:

Thank you for the opportunity to testify today on our work related to excess and underutilized federal real property held by civilian federal agencies, as well as our work on the military Base Realignment and Closure (BRAC) process. The federal government occupies more owned and leased buildings than it needs. In fiscal year 2009, 24 landholding agencies, including the Department of Defense (DOD), reported 45,190 underutilized buildings with a total of 341 million square feet, or 1,830 more such buildings than they reported the previous fiscal year. These underutilized buildings cost $1.66 billion annually to operate and are potentially valuable. The federal government also leases more property than is cost-efficient, resulting in millions of dollars of additional costs to the federal government. Since 2008, the General Services Administration (GSA) has leased more property than it owns[1]—more than 8,000 buildings—even though owning a federal building is often a more cost-effective way of meeting an agency's long-term space needs.[2] Because of these and other issues, we have designated the management of federal real property as a high-risk area.[3] On May 4, 2011, the administration proposed legislation, referred to as the Civilian Property Realignment Act (CPRA).[4] CPRA legislation has also been introduced in the House of Representatives.[5] Differences exist between the House bill and the administration's proposal. Throughout this statement, any reference to CPRA is the administration's proposed legislation.

At the request of this subcommittee, we have recently begun two new engagements related to federal real property management. The first will examine how federal agencies designate excess federal real property and what actions they are taking to better use remaining property. The second will examine the leasing costs incurred by the federal government.

Like GSA, DOD has faced long-term challenges in managing its portfolio of facilities, halting degradation of facilities, and reducing unneeded infrastructure to free up funds to better maintain the facilities that it still uses and to meet other needs. DOD's management of its support infrastructure is also on our high-risk list, in part because of challenges DOD faces in reducing excess and obsolete infrastructure.[6] As you know, DOD has been working through the BRAC process as one way to reduce the amount of unneeded property that it owns and leases. This process, which is designed to address the obstacles to matching needed infrastructure to the needed workforce and missions, may also be applicable to civilian real property management.

This statement discusses (1) progress the government has made toward addressing obstacles to federal real property management; (2) some of the challenges that remain for effective federal real property management and how the administration's proposed CPRA could be responsive to those challenges; and (3) key elements of the BRAC process that could be applied to expedite the disposal of unneeded civilian properties.

To address these objectives, we reviewed our previous work, reports by the interagency Federal Real Property Council (FRPC), and CPRA. We also visited an office and warehouse complex currently in the disposal process that included multiple types of real property at one address. This complex was judgmentally selected on the basis of its characteristics and its geographic proximity to our field office in Dallas, Texas. In addition, we reviewed the BRAC legislation and our reports on DOD's BRAC process and are currently monitoring BRAC 2005 implementation. We shared the relevant information in this statement with the Office of Management and Budget (OMB), GSA, and DOD officials. OMB and GSA did not provide comment. DOD provided technical comments which we incorporated as appropriate. We performed this work from May 2011 to June 2011 in accordance with generally accepted government auditing standards. Those standards require that we plan and perform the audit to obtain sufficient, appropriate evidence to provide a reasonable basis for our findings and conclusions based on our audit objectives. We believe that the evidence obtained provides a reasonable basis for our findings and conclusions based on our audit objectives.

BACKGROUND

The federal real property portfolio is vast and diverse, totaling more than 900,000 buildings and structures—including office buildings, warehouses, laboratories, hospitals, and family housing—and worth hundreds of billions of dollars. The six largest federal real property holding agencies— DOD; GSA; the U.S. Postal Service; and the Departments of Veterans Affairs (VA), Energy, and the Interior—occupy 87.6 percent of the total square footage in federal buildings. Overall, the federal government owns approximately 83 percent of this space and leases or otherwise manages the rest; however, these proportions vary by agency. For example GSA, the central leasing agent for most agencies, now leases more space than it owns.

The federal real property portfolio includes many properties the federal government no longer needs. In May 2011, the White House posted an interactive map of excess federal properties on its Web site,[7] noting that the map illustrates a sampling of over 7,000 buildings and structures currently designated as excess. These properties range from sheds to underutilized office buildings and empty warehouses. We visited an office and warehouse complex in Fort Worth, Texas that was listed on the Web site. Ten of the properties listed on the Web site as part of the Fort Worth complex were parceled together and auctioned in May 2011, but the sale is not yet final. The structures ranged from large warehouses to a concrete slab. (See fig. 1.) Work we are currently doing for this subcommittee on how federal agencies designate excess federal real property will include visits to other properties from around the country that are considered excess.

After we first designated federal real property as a high-risk area in 2003, the President issued Executive Order 13327 in February 2004, which established new federal property guidelines for 24 executive branch departments and agencies. Among other things, the executive order called for creating the interagency FRPC to develop guidance, collect best practices, and help agencies improve the management of their real property assets.

One of four large warehouses

Office building

Empty guard house structures

Figure 1. (Continued).

Concrete slab

Source: GAO.

Figure 1. Several Structures Auctioned by GSA in May 2011 in Ft. Worth, Texas.

DOD has undergone four BRAC rounds since 1988 and is currently implementing its fifth round.[8] Generally, the purpose of prior BRAC rounds was to generate savings to apply to other priorities, reduce property deemed excess to needs, and realign DOD's workload and workforce to achieve efficiencies in property management. As a result of the prior BRAC rounds in 1988, 1991, 1993, and 1995, DOD reported that it had reduced its domestic infrastructure, and transferred hundreds of thousands of acres of unneeded property to other federal and nonfederal entities. DOD data show that the department had generated an estimated $28.9 billion in net savings or cost avoidances from the prior four BRAC rounds through fiscal year 2003 and expects to save about $7 billion each year thereafter, which could be applied to other higher priority defense needs. These savings reflect money that DOD has estimated it would likely have spent to operate military bases had they remained open. However, we found that DOD's savings estimates are imprecise because the military services have not updated them regularly despite our prior reported concerns on this issue.[9] The 2005 BRAC round affected hundreds of locations across the country through 24 major closures, 24 major realignments, and 765 lesser actions, which also included terminating leases and consolidating various activities.[10] Legislation authorizing the 2005 BRAC round maintained requirements established for the three previous BRAC rounds that GAO provide a detailed analysis of DOD's recommendations and of the BRAC selection process. We submitted the results of our analysis in a 2005 report and testified before the BRAC Commission soon thereafter.[11] Since that time, we have published annual reports on the progress, challenges, and costs and savings of the 2005 round, in addition to numerous reports on other aspects of implementing the 2005 BRAC round.[12]

THE GOVERNMENT HAS ADOPTED A MORE STRATEGIC FOCUS TO IMPROVE REAL PROPERTY MANAGEMENT AND HAS TAKEN STEPS TO INCREASE DATA RELIABILITY

The administration and real-property-holding agencies have made progress in a number of areas since we designated federal real property as high risk in 2003. In 2003, we reported that despite the magnitude and complexity of real-property-related problems, there had been no governmentwide strategic focus on real property issues.[13] Not having a strategic focus can lead to ineffective decision making. As part of the government's efforts to strategically manage its real property, the administration established FRPC—a group composed of the OMB Controller and senior real property officers of landholding agencies—to support real property reform efforts. Through FRPC, the landholding agencies have also established asset management plans, standardized real property data reporting, and adopted various performance measures to track progress. The asset management plans are updated annually and help agencies take a more strategic approach to real property management by indicating how real property moves the agency's mission forward; outlining the agency's capital management plans; and describing how the agency plans to operate its facilities and dispose of unneeded real property, including listing current and future disposal plans. According to several member agencies, FRPC no longer meets regularly but remains a forum for agency coordination on real property issues and could serve a larger role in future real property management.

We also earlier reported that a lack of reliable real property data compounded real property management problems.[14] The governmentwide data maintained at that time were unreliable, out of date, and of limited value. In addition, certain key data that would be useful for budgeting and strategic management were not being maintained, such as data on space utilization, facility condition, historical significance, security, and age. We found that some of the major real-property-holding agencies faced challenges developing reliable data on their real property assets. We noted that reliable governmentwide and agency-specific real property data are critical for addressing real property management challenges. For example, better data would help the government determine whether assets are being used efficiently, make investment decisions, and identify unneeded properties.

In our February 2011 high-risk update, we reported that the federal government has taken numerous steps since 2003 to improve the completeness and reliability of its real property data.[15] FRPC, in conjunction with GSA, established the Federal Real Property Profile (FRPP) to meet a requirement in Executive Order 13327 for a single real property database that includes all real property under the control of executive branch agencies.[16] FRPP contains asset-level information submitted annually by agencies on 25 high-level data elements, including four performance measures that enable agencies to track progress in achieving property management objectives. In response to our 2007 recommendation to improve the reliability of FRPP data, OMB required, and agencies implemented, data validation plans that include procedures to verify that the data are accurate and complete.[17] Furthermore, GSA's Office of Governmentwide Policy (OGP), which administers the FRPP database, instituted a data validation process that precludes FRPP from accepting an agency's data until the data pass all established business rules and data checks. In our most recent analysis of the reliability of FRPP data, we found none of the previous basic problems, such as missing data or inexplicably large changes between years.[18] In addition, agencies continue to improve their real property data for their own purposes. From a governmentwide perspective, OGP has sufficient standards and processes in place for us to consider the 25 elements in FRPP as a database that is sufficiently reliable to describe the real property holdings of the federal government. Consequently, we removed the data element of real property management from our high-risk list this year.

CPRA COULD HELP AGENCIES ADDRESS UNDERLYING CHALLENGES TO DISPOSING OF UNNEEDED PROPERTY

The government now has a more strategic focus on real property issues and more reliable real property data, but problems related to unneeded property and leasing persist because the government has not addressed underlying legal and financial limitations and stakeholder influences. In our February 2011 high-risk update, we noted that the legal requirements agencies must adhere to before disposing of a property, such as requirements for screening and environmental cleanup, present a challenge to consolidating federal properties.[19] Currently, before GSA can dispose of a property that a federal agency no longer needs, it must offer the property to other federal agencies. If other federal agencies do not need the property, GSA must then make the property available to state and local governments and certain nonprofit organizations and institutions for public benefit uses, such as homeless shelters, educational facilities, or fire or police training centers.[20] As a result of this lengthy process, GSA's underutilized or excess properties may remain in an agency's possession for years and continue to accumulate maintenance and operations costs. We have also noted that the National Historic Preservation Act, as amended, requires agencies to manage historic properties under their control and jurisdiction and to consider the effects of their actions on historic preservation.[21] The average age of properties in GSA's portfolio is 46 years, and since properties more than 50 years old are eligible for historic designation, this issue will soon become critically important to GSA.

The costs of disposing of federal property further hamper some agencies' efforts to address their excess and underutilized real property problems. For example, federal agencies are required by law to assess and pay for any environmental cleanup that may be needed before disposing of a property[22]—a process that may require years of study and result in significant costs. In some cases, the cost of the environmental cleanup may exceed the costs of continuing to maintain the excess property in a shut-down status. The associated costs of complying with these legal requirements create disincentives to dispose of excess property.

Moreover, local stakeholders—including local governments, business interests, private real estate interests, private-sector construction and leasing firms, historic preservation organizations, various advocacy groups for citizens that benefit from federal programs, and the public in general— often view federal facilities as the physical face of the federal government in their communities. The interests of these multiple, and often competing stakeholders, may not always align with the most efficient use of government resources and can complicate real property decisions. For example, as we first reported in 2007, VA officials noted that stakeholders and constituencies, such as historic building advocates or local communities that want to maintain their relationship with VA, often prevent the agency from disposing of properties.[23] In 2003, we indicated that an independent commission or governmentwide task force might be necessary to help overcome stakeholder influences in real property decision making.

In 2007, we recommended that OMB, which is responsible for reviewing agencies' progress on federal real property management, assist agencies by developing an action plan to address the key problems associated with decisions related to unneeded real property, including stakeholder influences. OMB agreed with the recommendation. The administration's recently proposed legislative framework, CPRA, is somewhat responsive to our recommendation in that it addresses legal and financial limitations, as well as stakeholder influences in real property decision making.

- With the goal of streamlining the disposal process, CPRA provides for an independent board to determine which properties it considers would be the most appropriate for public benefit uses.[24] This streamlined process could reduce both the time it takes for the government to dispose of property and the amount the government pays to maintain property.
- To provide financial assistance to the agencies, CPRA establishes an Asset Proceeds and Space Management Fund from which funds could be transferred to reimburse an agency for necessary costs associated with disposing of property.[25] Reimbursing agencies for the costs they incur would potentially facilitate the disposal process.
- To address stakeholder influences, the independent board established under CPRA would, among other things, recommend federal properties for disposal or consolidation after receiving recommendations from civilian landholding agencies and would independently review the agencies' recommendations. Grouping all disposal and consolidation decisions into one set of proposals that Congress would consider in its entirety could help to limit local stakeholder influences at any individual site.

CPRA does not explicitly address the government's overreliance on leasing. In 2008, we found that decisions to lease selected federal properties were not always driven by cost-effectiveness considerations.[26] For example, we estimated that the decision to lease the Federal Bureau of Investigation's field office in Chicago, Illinois, instead of constructing a building the government would own, cost about $40 million more over 30 years. GSA officials noted that the limited availability of upfront capital was one of the reasons that prevented ownership at that time. Federal budget scorekeeping rules require the full cost of construction to be recorded up front in the budget, whereas only the annual lease payments plus cancellation costs need to be recorded for operating leases. In April 2007 and January 2008, we recommended that OMB develop a strategy to reduce agencies' reliance on costly leasing where ownership would result in long-term savings.[27] We noted that such a strategy could identify the conditions under which leasing is an acceptable alternative, include an analysis of real property budget scoring issues, and provide an assessment of viable alternatives. OMB concurred with this recommendation but has not yet developed a strategy to reduce agencies' reliance on leasing. One of CPRA's purposes—to realign civilian real property by consolidating, colocating, and reconfiguring space to increase efficiency—could help to reduce the government's overreliance on leasing. Our current work examines the efficiency of the federal government's real property lease management in more detail.

KEY ELEMENTS OF DOD'S BRAC PROCESS THAT COULD EXPEDITE THE DISPOSAL OF UNNEEDED CIVILIAN PROPERTIES

DOD has undergone five BRAC rounds to realign DOD's workload to achieve efficiencies and savings in property management, including reducing excess properties. The BRAC process, much like CPRA, was designed to address obstacles to closures or realignments, thus permitting DOD to close or realign installations and its missions to better use its facilities and generate savings. Certain key elements of DOD's process for closing and realigning its installations may be applicable to the realignment of real property governmentwide. Some of these key elements include establishing goals, developing criteria for evaluating closures and realignments, developing a structural plan for applying selection criteria, estimating the costs and savings anticipated from implementing recommendations, establishing a structured process for obtaining and analyzing data, and involving the audit community.

DOD's 2005 BRAC Process

DOD's BRAC process was designed to address certain challenges to base closures or realignments, including stakeholder interests, thereby permitting the department to realign its missions to better use its facilities, generate savings, and sometimes also resulting in the disposal of property. The most recent defense base closure and realignment round followed a historical analytical framework, carrying many elements of the process forward or building upon lessons learned from the department's four previous rounds. DOD used a logical, reasoned, and well-documented process.[28] In addition, we have identified lessons learned from DOD's 1988, 1991, 1993, and 1995 rounds,[29] and we have begun an effort to assess lessons learned from the 2005 BRAC round.

DOD's 2005 BRAC process consisted of activities that followed a series of statutorily prescribed steps,[30] including:

- Congress established clear time frames for implementation;
- DOD developed options for closure or realignment recommendations;
- BRAC Commission independently reviewed DOD's proposed recommendations;
- President reviewed and approved the BRAC recommendations; and
- Congress did not disapprove of the recommendations and thus they became binding.

Key Elements that DOD Used to Develop Its 2005 BRAC Recommendations that Could Benefit a Civilian Real Property Closure or Realignment Process

In developing its recommendations for the BRAC Commission, DOD relied on certain elements in its process that Congress may wish to consider as it evaluates the administration's proposed legislation for disposing of or realigning civilian real property, as follows:

Establish Goals for the Process

The Secretary of Defense emphasized the importance of transforming the military to make it more efficient as part of the 2005 BRAC round. Other goals for the 2005 BRAC process included fostering jointness among the four military services, reducing excess infrastructure, and producing savings. Prior rounds were more about reducing excess infrastructure and producing savings.

Develop Criteria for Evaluating Closures and Realignments

DOD initially proposed eight selection criteria, which were made available for public comments via the Federal Register. Ultimately, Congress enacted the eight final BRAC selection criteria in law [31] and specified that four selection criteria, known as the "military value criteria," were to be given priority in developing closure and realignment recommendations. The primary military value criteria include such considerations as an installation's current and future mission capabilities and the impact on operational readiness of the total force; the availability and condition of land, facilities, and associated airspace at both existing and potentially receiving locations; the ability to accommodate a surge in the force and future total force requirements at both existing and potentially receiving locations; and costs of operations and personnel implications. In addition, Congress specified that in developing its recommendations, DOD was to apply "other criteria," such as the costs and savings associated with a recommendation; the economic impact on existing communities near the installations; the ability of the infrastructure in existing and potential communities to support forces, missions, and personnel; and environmental impact. Further, Congress required that the Secretary of Defense develop and submit to Congress a force structure plan that described the probable size of major military units—for example, divisions, ships, and air wings—needed to address probable threats to national security based on the Secretary's assessment of those threats for the 20-year period beginning in 2005, along with a comprehensive inventory of global military installations.[32] In authorizing the 2005 BRAC round, Congress specified that the Secretary of Defense publish a list of recommendations for the closure and realignment of military installations inside the United States based on the statutorily-required 20-year force-structure plan and infrastructure inventory, and on the selection criteria.

Estimate Costs and Savings to Implement Closure and Realignment Recommendations

To address the cost and savings criteria, DOD developed and used the Cost of Base Realignment Actions model (COBRA) a quantitative tool that DOD has used since the 1988 BRAC round to provide consistency in potential cost, savings, and return-oninvestment estimates for closure and realignment options. We reviewed the COBRA model as part of our review of the 2005 and prior BRAC rounds and found it to be a generally reasonable estimator for comparing potential costs and savings among alternatives. As with any model, the quality of the output is a direct function of the input data. Also, DOD's

COBRA model relies to a large extent on standard factors and averages and does not represent budget quality estimates that are developed once BRAC decisions are made and detailed implementation plans are developed. Nonetheless, the financial information provides important input into the selection process as decision makers weigh the financial implications—along with military value criteria and other considerations—in arriving at final decisions about the suitability of various closure and realignment options. However, according to our assessment of the 2005 BRAC round, actual costs and savings were different from estimates.[33]

Establish an Organizational Structure

The Office of the Secretary of Defense emphasized the need for joint cross-service groups to analyze common business-oriented functions. For the 2005 BRAC round, as for the 1993 and 1995 rounds, these joint cross-service groups performed analyses and developed closure and realignment options in addition to those developed by the military services. In contrast, our evaluation of DOD's 1995 BRAC round indicated that few cross-service recommendations were made, in part because of the lack of high-level leadership to encourage consolidations across the services' functions.[34] In the 1995 BRAC round, the joint cross-service groups submitted options through the military services for approval, but few were approved. The number of approved recommendations that the joint cross-service groups developed significantly increased in the 2005 BRAC round. This was in part, because high-level leadership ensured that the options were approved not by the military services but rather by a DOD senior-level group.

Establish a Common Analytical Framework

To ensure that the selection criteria were consistently applied, the Office of the Secretary of Defense, the military services, and the seven joint cross-service groups first performed a capacity analysis of facilities and functions in which all installations received some basic capacity questions according to DOD. Before developing the candidate recommendations, DOD's capacity analysis relied on data calls to hundreds of locations to obtain certified data to assess such factors as maximum potential capacity, current capacity, current usage, and excess capacity. Then, the military services and joint cross-service groups performed a military value analysis for the facilities and functions based on primary military value criteria, which included a facility's or function's current and future mission capabilities, physical condition, ability to accommodate future needs, and cost of operations.

Involve the Audit Community to Better Ensure Data Accuracy

The DOD Inspector General and military service audit agencies played key roles in identifying data limitations, pointing out needed corrections, and improving the accuracy of the data used in the process. In their oversight roles, the audit organizations, who had access to relevant information and officials as the process evolved, helped to improve the accuracy of the data used in the BRAC process and thus strengthened the quality and integrity of the data used to develop closure and realignment recommendations. For example, the auditors worked to ensure certified information was used for BRAC analysis, and reviewed other facets of the process, including the various internal control plans, the COBRA model, and other modeling and analytical tools that were used in the development of recommendations.

There are a number of important similarities between BRAC and a civilian process as proposed in the administration's CPRA. As a similarity, both BRAC and CPRA employ the all-or-nothing approach to disposals and consolidations, meaning that once the final list is approved by the independent commission or board, it must be accepted or rejected as a whole. Another important similarity is that both the BRAC and proposed CPRA processes call for an independent board or commission to review recommendations.

A key difference between BRAC and the administration's proposed CPRA is that while the BRAC process placed the Secretary of Defense in a central role to review and submit candidate recommendations to the independent board, CPRA does not provide for any similar central role for civilian agencies. The BRAC process required the Secretary of Defense to develop and submit recommendations to the BRAC Commission for review. In this role, the Office of the Secretary of Defense reviewed and revised the various candidate recommendations developed by the four military services and the seven separate joint cross service groups. In contrast, the administration's proposed CPRA does not place any official or organization in such a central role to review and submit the recommendations proposed by various federal agencies to the independent board for assessment and approval. Another key difference between BRAC and CPRA is the time period in which the commission will be in existence. CPRA, as proposed by the administration, is a continuing commission which will provide recommendations twice a year for 12 years, whereas, the BRAC Commission convened only for those years in which it was authorized. For example, after the most recent 2005 BRAC round, the Commission terminated by law in April 2006. However, we believe the need for a phased approach involving multiple rounds of civilian property realignments is warranted given it may take several BRAC-like rounds to complete the disposals and consolidations of civilian real property owned and leased by many disparate agencies including GSA, VA, Department of the Interior, Department of Energy, and others.

In closing, the government has made strides toward strategically managing its real property and improving its real property planning and data over the last 10 years, but those efforts have not yet led to sufficient reductions in excess property and overreliance on leasing. DOD's experience with BRAC could help the process move forward to dispose of unneeded civilian real property and generate savings for the taxpayer.

Chairman Carper, Ranking Member Brown, and Members of the Subcommittee, this concludes our prepared statement. We will be pleased to answer any questions that you may have at this time.

End Notes

[1] In this testimony, we refer to property that is owned by the federal government and under the control and custody of GSA as GSA-owned property.

[2] GAO, *Federal Real Property: Strategy Needed to Address Agencies' Long-standing Reliance on Leasing*, GAO-08-197 (Washington, D.C.: Jan. 24, 2008).

[3] *High-Risk Series: An Update*, GAO-11-278 (Washington, D.C.: February 2011).

[4] Letter from Jacob J. Lew, Director, Office of Management and Budget, to The Honorable Joseph R. Biden, President of the Senate (May 4, 2011) (available at www.whitehouse.gov/omb/financial (last visited June 1, 2011)).

[5] H.R. 1734, 112th Cong. (2011).

[6] GAO-11-278.

[7] See http://www.whitehouse.gov/issues (last visited June 1, 2011).

[8] The first round in 1988 was authorized by the Defense Authorization Amendments and Base Closure and Realignment Act, Pub. L. No. 100-526, Title II (1988) (as amended). Subsequently, additional BRAC rounds were completed in 1991, 1993, and 1995 as authorized by the Defense Base Closure and Realignment Act of 1990, Pub. L. No. 101-510, Title XXIX (1990) (as amended). The latest round—BRAC 2005—was authorized by the National Defense Authorization Act for Fiscal Year 2002, Pub. L. No. 107-107, Title XXX (2001) (as amended).

[9] In addition, we have also reported that we believe that DOD's net annual recurring savings estimates are overstated because they include savings from eliminating military personnel positions without corresponding decreases in personnel end-strength. DOD disagrees with our position. GAO, *Military Bases: Analysis of DOD's 1995 Process and Recommendations for Closure and Realignment*, GAO/NSIAD-95-133 (Washington, D.C.: Apr. 14, 1995) and *Military Base Realignments and Closures: Estimated Costs Have Increased and Estimated Savings Have Decreased*, GAO-08-314T (Washington, D.C.: Dec. 12, 2007).

[10] DOD defines a major closure as a closure where plant replacement values exceed $100 million and major realignments as actions with net losses of 400 or more military and civilian personnel.

[11] GAO, *Military Bases: Analysis of DOD's 2005 Selection Process and Recommendations for Base Closures and Realignments*, GAO-05-785 (Washington: D.C.: July 1, 2005) and *Military Bases: Observations on the 2005 Base Realignment and Closure Selection Process and Recommendations*, GAO-05-905 (Washington, DC: July 18, 2005).

[12] See, for example, GAO, *Military Base Realignments and Closures: DOD Is Taking Steps to Mitigate Challenges, but Is Not Fully Reporting Some Additional Costs*, GAO-10-725R (Washington, D.C.: July 21, 2010) and *Military Base Realignments and Closures: Estimated Costs Have Increased While Savings Estimates Have Decreased Since Fiscal Year 2009*, GAO-10-98R (Washington, D.C.: Nov. 13, 2009).

[13] GAO, *High-Risk Series: Federal Real Property*, GAO-03-122 (Washington, D.C.: January 2003).

[14] GAO-03-122.

[15] GAO-11-278.

[16] 40 U.S.C. § 524.

[17] GAO, *Federal Real Property: Progress Made Toward Addressing Problems, but Underlying Obstacles Continue to Hamper Reform*, GAO-07-349 (Washington, D.C.: Apr. 13, 2007).

[18] GAO-11-278.

[19] GAO-11-278.

[20] 42 U.S.C. § 11411; 40 U.S.C. §§ 550, 553.

[21] 16 U.S.C. §§ 470f, 470h-2.

[22] 42 U.S.C. § 9620.

[23] GAO-07-349.

[24] The board would be composed of seven members appointed by the President. At least two members must have experience in the private sector and at least two members must have experience in the public sector.

[25] The Asset Management Proceeds and Space Management Fund, established by CPRA, is funded with appropriations, gross proceeds received from the disposal of civilian real property pursuant to recommendations by the Board, as well as certain net proceeds received from the disposal of civilian real properties pursuant to recommendations by the Board.

[26] GAO-08-197.

[27] GAO-07-349 and GAO-08-197.

[28] GAO-05-785.

[29] GAO, *Military Bases: Lessons Learned From Prior Base Closure Rounds*, NSIAD-97-151 (Washington, D.C.: July 25, 1997).

[30] See, GAO, *Federal Real Property: Progress Made on Planning and Data, but Unneeded Owned and Leased Facilities Remain,* GAO-11-520T (Washington, D.C.: Apr. 6, 2011).

[31] Section 2832 of the Ronald W. Reagan National Defense Authorization Act for Fiscal Year 2005 (Pub. L. No. 108-375 (2004)).

[32] Section 3001 of the National Defense Authorization Act for Fiscal Year 2002 (Pub. L. No. 107-107 (2001)), amended the Defense Base Closure and Realignment Act of 1990 (Pub. L. No. 101-510 (1990)) to, among other things, require DOD to develop a 20-year force structure plan as the basis for its 2005 BRAC analysis to include the probable end strength levels and major military force units needed to meet the probable threats identified by the Secretary of Defense.

[33] As we reported in November 2009 (GAO-10-98R), BRAC one-time implementation costs rose to almost $35 billion in fiscal year 2010 compared with DOD's initial estimate of $21

billion in 2005. Similarly, net annual recurring savings dropped to $3.9 billion in fiscal year 2010 compared with the $4.2 billion DOD estimated in 2005.

[34] NSIAD-97-151.

In: Federal Real Property Disposition   ISBN: 978-1-62100-048-8
Editor: Iain D. Haque   © 2012 Nova Science Publishers, Inc.

Chapter 3

FEDERAL REAL PROPERTY: THE GOVERNMENT FACES CHALLENGES TO DISPOSING OF UNNEEDED BUILDINGS[*]

United States Government Accountability Office

WHY GAO DID THIS STUDY

The federal real property portfolio, comprising over 900,000 buildings and structures and worth hundreds of billions of dollars, presents management challenges. In January 2003, GAO designated the management of federal real property as a high-risk area in part due to the presence of unneeded property. The Office of Management and Budget (OMB) is responsible for reviewing agencies' progress on federal real property management. The General Services Administration (GSA), often referred to as the federal government's landlord, controls more square feet of buildings than any other civilian federal agency. GSA funds real property acquisition, operation, maintenance, and disposal through the rent it collects from tenant agencies that is deposited into the Federal Buildings Fund (FBF). This testimony discusses (1) the scope and costs of the excess real property held by GSA and other federal agencies; and (2) the challenges GSA and other federal agencies face in disposing of excess and underutilized real property. GAO analyzed GSA data from a centralized

---

[*] This is an edited, reformatted and augmented version of the United States Government Accountability Office publication GAO-11-370T, dated February 10, 2011.

real property database, reviewed GSA real property plans and previous GAO reports, and interviewed GSA and OMB officials.

WHAT GAO FOUND

The federal government holds many excess and underutilized properties that cost billions of dollars annually to operate. Excess properties are buildings that agencies have identified as having no further program use, and underutilized properties serve a program purpose that could be satisfied with only a portion of the property. In fiscal year 2009, 24 federal agencies including the Department of Defense reported 45,190 underutilized buildings that cost $1.66 billion annually to operate. GSA specifically holds 282 excess or otherwise underutilized buildings that cost $93 million annually to operate. Underutilized buildings represent the first places to look for possible consolidations that could, in turn, allow GSA to dispose of additional properties. Excess and underutilized properties erode the viability of FBF by forcing GSA to pay for buildings for which it gets no return. The viability of FBF is essential to ensuring that GSA is able to respond to changing government real estate needs over the coming years and make sound investment decisions. A June 2010 Presidential Memorandum continued government efforts to dispose of unneeded properties by establishing a new governmentwide target of $3 billion savings through disposals and other methods by the end of fiscal year 2012.

The problem of excess and underutilized property is exacerbated by a number of factors that impede the government's ability to efficiently dispose of unneeded property. First, numerous stakeholders, including local governments, private real estate interests, and advocacy groups, have an interest in how the federal government carries out its real property acquisition, management, and disposal practices. These competing interests, that often view government buildings as the physical face of the federal government in local communities, can build barriers to property disposal. In 2007, GAO recommended that OMB develop an action plan to address the effects of stakeholder interests but it has yet to be implemented. Second, the complex legal environment has a significant impact on real property decisionmaking and may not lead to economically rational outcomes. GSA's ability to effectively dispose of its unneeded property can also be hampered by its lengthy disposal process, which is legislatively mandated and includes requirements, such as determining whether the property can be used by other federal agencies, for homeless assistance, and for the public benefit. For example, GSA continues to hold numerous buildings that have been listed as excess for years. The lengthy disposal process may inhibit GSA's ability to achieve cost savings under the Presidential Memorandum by the 2012 deadline.

STATEMENT OF DAVID J. WISE, DIRECTOR, PHYSICAL INFRASTRUCTURE ISSUES

Mr. Chairman and Members of the Subcommittee:

Thank you for the opportunity to testify today on our work related to federal real property and in particular, the issue of excess and underutilized property held by the General Services Administration (GSA) and other agencies. As you know, since 1990, we have periodically reported on government operations that we identify as "high risk." In January 2003, we designated the management of federal real property as a high-risk area, in part because of excess and underutilized property. Other reasons included over-reliance on leasing and the challenges associated with protecting government assets from terrorism. Later this month, we plan to issue an update on the status of these issues as part of our update to the high-risk series. My testimony today will discuss (1) the scope and costs of excess and underutilized real property held by GSA and other federal agencies; and (2) the challenges GSA and other federal agencies face in disposing of excess and underutilized real property. To address these objectives, we analyzed GSA data from the Federal Real Property Profile, a centralized real property database, for fiscal year 2009. We determined the data were sufficiently reliable for our purposes through data testing and interviews with government officials responsible for submitting and maintaining the data. We also reviewed GSA real property plans and previous GAO reports, and interviewed GSA and Office of Management and Budget (OMB) officials. We performed this work from June 2010 to February 2011 in accordance with generally accepted government auditing standards. Those standards require that we plan and perform the audit to obtain sufficient, appropriate evidence to provide a reasonable basis for our findings and conclusions based on our audit objectives. We believe that the evidence obtained provides a reasonable basis for our findings and conclusions based on our audit objectives.

BACKGROUND

The federal government's real property portfolio presents significant management challenges and, in many cases, reflects an infrastructure based on the business model and technological environment of the 1950s. In identifying governmentwide real property management as a high risk issue, we found that many government real property assets are no longer effectively aligned with, or are responsive to, agencies' changing missions. As a result, many are no longer needed. These can include excess properties, which agencies have identified as having no further program use, and underutilized properties, which serve a program purpose that could be satisfied with only a portion of the property. [1] As we have previously reported, excess and underutilized properties present significant risks to federal agencies because they are costly to maintain and could be put to more cost-beneficial uses or sold to generate revenue for the government.

The federal real property portfolio includes buildings used as offices, warehouses, schools, laboratories, hospitals, and family housing and land. Over 30 federal agencies control real property assets—including both facilities and land—in the United States and abroad. In fiscal year 2009, the federal inventory included over 3 billion square feet of building space and over 900,000 buildings and structures that are worth hundreds of billions of dollars. Approximately 83 percent of federally occupied space is owned by the federal government, while the remaining amount is leased or otherwise managed.

GSA, often referred to as the federal government's landlord, controls more square feet of buildings—most of which it leases to other federal agencies and entities—than any other civilian federal agency. Figure 1 illustrates GSA's ten largest tenants by rent, ranked by total square feet.

GSA provides a range of real estate services to its tenant agencies, including acquisition, operations, maintenance, and disposal of property which it finances through a revolving fund called the Federal Buildings Fund (FBF). GSA deposits the rent it collects from tenant agencies into FBF, which it then proposes to spend as part of the President's annual budget request to Congress. In fiscal year 2009, GSA collected over $8.5 billion in rent, of which almost three quarters came from its 10 largest tenants. In 2005, GSA received the authority to deposit the net proceeds for its property dispositions directly into FBF.[2] The disposal of 133 GSA-controlled properties from fiscal years 2005 through 2009 generated almost $200 million in net proceeds for FBF.

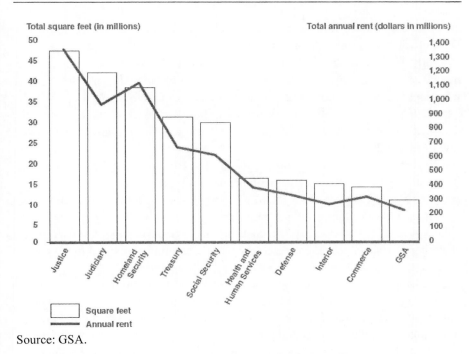

Source: GSA.

Figure 1. Top 10 GSA Tenants by Rent, Ranked by Total Square Feet.

THE GOVERNMENT HAS MANY EXCESS AND UNDERUTILIZED BUILDINGS, COSTING BILLIONS TO OPERATE

In fiscal year 2009, agencies reported 45,190 underutilized buildings with a total of 341 million square feet, an increase of 1,830 such buildings from the previous fiscal year. These underutilized buildings accounted for $1.66 billion in annual operating costs. These totals include buildings reported by 24 agencies, the largest of which is the Department of Defense.[3] Underutilized buildings represent the first places to look for possible consolidations that could, in turn, allow agencies to dispose of such properties.

GSA also has many properties it no longer needs. In fiscal year 2009 (the most recent year for which data are available), GSA reported having 282 excess or otherwise underutilized buildings. These buildings, which include offices and warehouses, cost about $93 million a year to operate. They encompass about 18 million square feet and are located in 43 states and the District of Columbia. Approximately 70 percent of these properties are federally owned which GSA controls and the rest are leased from private owners. For example, GSA's excess properties include an office and warehouse complex, covering about 1 million square feet in Fort Worth, Texas. GSA spent about $1.3 million in fiscal year 2009 to operate this complex. According to GSA officials, these properties are planned for public sale in spring 2011.

Excess and underutilized properties erode FBF, potentially threatening its financial viability. GSA funds maintenance and repair costs to operate excess facilities from FBF. It must then pay to operate and maintain unneeded buildings without gaining tenant rent in return to cover these expenses. The viability of FBF is essential to ensuring that GSA is able to respond to changing government real estate needs over the coming years and make sound investment decisions.

The administration recently built upon the previous administration's focus on the need to dispose of unneeded properties throughout the government. In a June 2010 Presidential Memorandum to federal agencies, the administration stated that the federal government, as the largest property owner and energy user in the United States, wastes both taxpayer dollars and energy resources to maintain unneeded real estate. The memo established a new target of saving $3 billion governmentwide through disposals and other methods by the end of fiscal year 2012. The memo directed that these cost savings be derived from increased proceeds from the sale of assets and reduced operating, maintenance, and energy expenses from disposals or other space consolidation efforts, including leases that are ended.

CHALLENGES IMPEDE THE DISPOSAL OF EXCESS REAL PROPERTY

As we have previously reported, the problem of excess and underutilized property is exacerbated by a number of factors that impede the government's ability to efficiently dispose of unneeded property.[4] For example, numerous stakeholders have an interest in how the federal government carries out its real property acquisition, management, and disposal practices. These include local governments; business interests in the communities where the assets are located; private sector construction and leasing firms; historic preservation organizations; various advocacy groups for citizens that benefit from or use federal programs; and the public in general, which often view the facilities as the physical face of the federal government in local communities. These competing stakeholder interests can build barriers to real property disposals. In 2007 we recommended that OMB, which is responsible for reviewing agencies' progress on federal real property management, could assist agencies by developing an action plan to address key problems associated with unneeded real property, including reducing the effect of stakeholder interests in real property decisions.[5] OMB agreed with the recommendation but has yet to implement it. OMB officials said they are unsure how to reduce the impact of stakeholder influence on real property decisions.

The complex legal environment also has a significant impact on real property decisionmaking and may not lead to economically rational outcomes. Not all agencies are authorized to retain proceeds from property sales. In addition, federal agencies are required by law to assess and pay for any environmental cleanup that may be needed before disposing of a property—a process that may require years of study and result in significant costs. In some cases, the cost of the environment cleanup may exceed the costs of continuing to maintain the excess property in a shut-down status. We have also noted that the National Historic Preservation Act, as amended, requires agencies to manage historic properties under their control and jurisdiction and to consider the effects of their actions on historic preservation.[6] The issue of historic preservation will become of critical importance to GSA since properties more than 50 years old are eligible for historic designation and GSA's portfolio has an average age of 46 years.

GSA's ability to effectively dispose of its unneeded property can also be hampered by its lengthy disposal process, which is legislatively mandated (see Fig. 2). This process includes screening other federal agencies for possible continued federal need. In addition, GSA has the authority to retain the net proceeds from the sale of real property but must, before offering property for sale, follow requirements under Title 40 of the United States Code and the McKinney-Vento Homeless Assistance Act.[7] Some of these steps many result in the property being disposed of with no proceeds. For example, under the public benefit conveyance program, state or local governments and certain tax exempt nonprofit organizations can obtain surplus real property for public uses such as homeless centers, educational facilities, or fire or police training centers. These steps in the disposal process serve as opportunities for stakeholder input and invite opportunities for stakeholder conflicts, such as conflicting views from local community groups for how best to use excess properties.

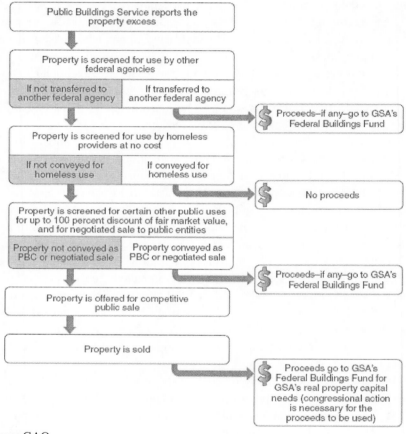

Source: GAO.

Figure 2. GSA's Legislatively Mandated Process for Selling Excess Property.

The fact that GSA's underutilized or excess properties, even those slated for disposal, may remain in GSA's possession for years, provides further evidence of GSA's difficulties in this area. For example, we previously reported on a GSA-created list of vacant and underutilized GSA properties as of October 1, 2002, including some which GSA had initiated actions for disposal.[8] These properties slated for disposal included a collection of federal building properties at one location in Alameda, California, and 6 federal buildings in Kansas City, Missouri. At the time, the properties in Kansas City were entirely vacant. In fiscal year 2009, GSA reported that the agency owned excess properties at these same locations totaling about 646,000 square feet and costing a total of around $182,000 annually to operate. While GSA has attempted to dispose of these excess properties, the agency has had to continue to maintain the properties over the past 7 years. The lengthy disposal process may therefore limit GSA's ability to achieve cost savings under the Presidential Memorandum. GSA officials said they are unlikely to have enough time to identify additional properties for disposal, complete the disposals, and achieve the cost savings by the 2012 deadline included in the Presidential Memorandum. Instead, officials said that they will have to rely on cost savings achieved from previously planned disposals in the "pipeline" and through other sources of savings, such as improvements in energy efficiency.

In closing, the government has many excess and underutilized properties that cost billions of dollars each year to maintain. Despite efforts to reduce this inventory, multiple obstacles remain that preclude quick and easy solutions. Until these obstacles are overcome, this issue will remain high risk.

Thank you, Mr. Chairman, that concludes my statement. I will be pleased to answer any questions that you or other Members of the Subcommittee may have at this time.

For further information on this testimony, please contact David Wise at (202) 512-2834 or wised@gao.gov. Contact points for our Congressional Relations and Public Affairs offices may be found on the last page of this statement. Individuals making key contributions to this testimony were Keith Cunningham, Assistant Director; Lynnelle Evans; Colin Fallon; Erik Kjeldgaard; Emily Larson; Susan Michal-Smith; Minette Richardson; and Swati Thomas.

End Notes

[1] Utilization is obtained by calculating a ratio of occupancy to current design capacity. An office is considered underutilized if this ratio is less than 75 percent. A warehouse is considered underutilized if this ratio is less than 50 percent.

[2] Section 412 of P.L. No. 108-447, 118 Stat. 2809, 3529 (2004).

[3] The Department of Defense accounted for 64% of the total building square feet held by these 24 agencies in fiscal year 2009.

[4] GAO, *Federal Real Property: Progress Made Toward Addressing Problems, but Underlying Obstacles Continue to Hamper Reform,* GAO-07-349 (Washington, D.C.; April 2007).

[5] GAO-07-349.

[6] 16 U.S.C. § 470 et seq.

[7] U.S.C. § 11411.

[8] GAO, *Federal Real Property: Vacant and Underutilized Properties at GSA, VA, and USPS,* GAO-03-747 (Washington, D.C.; Aug. 2003). This list also included some of the properties in Forth Worth previously mentioned.

In: Federal Real Property Disposition   ISBN: 978-1-62100-048-8
Editor: Iain D. Haque   © 2012 Nova Science Publishers, Inc.

Chapter 4

FEDERAL REAL PROPERTY:
AN UPDATE ON HIGH RISK ISSUES[*]

United States Government Accountability Office

WHY GAO DID THIS STUDY

In January 2003, GAO designated federal real property as a high-risk area because of long-standing problems with excess and underutilized property, deteriorating facilities, unreliable real property data, over-reliance on costly leasing, and security challenges. In January 2009, GAO found that agencies have taken some positive steps to address real property issues but that some of the core problems that led to the designation of this area as high risk persist.

This testimony focuses on (1) progress made by major real property-holding agencies to strategically manage real property, (2) ongoing problems GAO has identified in recent work regarding agencies' efforts to address real property issues, and (3) underlying obstacles GAO has identified through prior work as hampering agencies' real property reform efforts governmentwide.

This testimony is largely based on GAO's extensive body of work on real property high-risk issues, including reports on efforts by the Office of Management and Budget (OMB) and executive branch agencies to address real property issues. No new recommendations are being made.

---

[*] This is an edited, reformatted and augmented version of the United States Government Accountability Office publication GAO-09-801T, dated July 15, 2009.

WHAT GAO FOUND

OMB and real property-holding agencies have made progress in strategically managing real property. In response to an administration reform initiative and related executive order, agencies have, among other things, established asset management plans, standardized data, and adopted performance measures. According to OMB, the federal government disposed of excess real property valued at $1 billion in fiscal year 2008, bringing the total to over $8 billion since fiscal year 2004. OMB also reported success in developing a comprehensive database of federal real property assets and implemented a GAO recommendation to improve the reliability of the data in this database by developing a framework to validate these data. GAO also found that the Veterans Administration has made significant progress in reducing underutilized space. In another report, GAO found that six agencies reviewed have processes in place to prioritize maintenance and repair items.

While these actions represent positive steps, some of the long-standing problems that led GAO to designate this area as high risk persist. Although GAO's work over the years has shown that building ownership often costs less than operating leases, especially for long term space needs, in 2008, the General Services Administration (GSA), which acts as the government's leasing agent, leased more property than it owned for the first time. Given GSA's ongoing reliance on leasing, it is critical that GSA manage its leasing activities effectively. However, in January 2007, GAO identified numerous areas that warranted improvement in GSA's implementation of four contracts for national broker services for its leasing program. GSA has implemented 7 of GAO's 11 recommendations to improve these contracting efforts. Although GAO is encouraged by GSA's actions on these recommendations, GAO has not evaluated their impact. Moreover, in more recent work, GAO has continued to find that the government's real property data are not always reliable and agencies continue to retain excess property and face challenges from repair and maintenance backlogs. Regarding security, GAO testified on July 8, 2009, that preliminary results show that the ability of the Federal Protective Service (FPS), which provides security services for about 9,000 GSA facilities, to protect federal facilities is hampered by weaknesses in its contract security guard program. Among other things, GAO investigators carrying the components for an improvised explosive device successfully passed undetected through security checkpoints monitored by FPS's guards at each of the 10 federal facilities where GAO conducted covert testing.

As GAO has reported in the past, real property management problems have been exacerbated by deep-rooted obstacles that include competing stakeholder interests, various budgetary and legal limitations, and weaknesses in agencies' capital planning. While reforms to date are positive, the new administration and Congress will be challenged to sustain reform momentum and reach consensus on how such obstacles should be addressed.

STATEMENT OF MARK L. GOLDSTEIN, DIRECTOR, PHYSICAL INFRASTRUCTURE ISSUES

Madam Chair and Members of the Subcommittee:

We welcome the opportunity to provide this update on our recent work on issues that led us to designate federal real property as a high-risk area. As you know, in January 2003, we designated federal real property a high-risk area because of long-standing problems with excess and underutilized property, deteriorating facilities, unreliable real property data, overreliance on costly leasing, and building security challenges.[1] As we have reported as part of the high-risk series, the federal real property portfolio largely reflects a business model and the technological and transportation environment of the 1950s. Many federal real property assets are no longer needed; others are not effectively aligned with, or responsive to, agencies' changing missions. We issued our latest update on this area in January 2009, finding that agencies have taken some positive steps to address real property issues but that some of the core problems that led to our designation of this area as high risk persist.[2] My testimony today is based on our extensive body of work related to these issues.[3] We also spoke with officials at the Office of Management and Budget (OMB) and the General Services Administration (GSA) to update our information on agencies' efforts to address our prior recommendations, and we reviewed recently-introduced initiatives related to agencies' real property disposal authorities.[4] My testimony focuses on (1) progress made by major real property-holding agencies to strategically manage real property,[5] (2) ongoing problems we have identified in recent work regarding agencies' efforts to address real property issues, and (3) underlying obstacles we have identified through prior work as hampering agencies' real property reform efforts governmentwide. We conducted our work in Washington, D.C., in June and July 2009 in accordance with generally accepted government auditing standards. Those standards require that we plan and perform the audit to obtain sufficient, appropriate evidence to provide a reasonable basis for our findings and conclusions based on our audit objectives. We believe that the evidence obtained provides a reasonable basis for our findings and conclusions based on our audit objectives.

UNDER REAL PROPERTY INITIATIVE, AGENCIES HAVE TAKEN ACTIONS TO STRATEGICALLY MANAGE REAL PROPERTY AND ADDRESS SOME LONG-STANDING PROBLEMS

Major real property-holding agencies and OMB have made progress toward strategically managing federal real property. In April 2007, we found that in response to the President's Management Agenda (PMA) real property initiative and a related executive order, agencies covered under the executive order had, among other things, designated senior real property officers, established asset management plans, standardized real property data reporting, and adopted various performance measures to track progress.[6] The administration had also established a Federal Real Property Council (FRPC) that guides reform efforts.

Under the real property initiative, OMB has been evaluating the status and progress of agencies' real property management improvement efforts since the third quarter of fiscal year 2004 using a quarterly scorecard[7] that color codes agencies' progress—green for success, yellow for mixed results, and red for unsatisfactory. As Figure 1 shows, according to OMB's analysis, many of these agencies have made progress in accurately accounting for, maintaining, and managing their real property assets so as to efficiently meet their goals and objectives. As of the first quarter of 2009, 10 of the 15 agencies evaluated had achieved green status. According to OMB, the agencies achieving green status have established 3-year timelines for meeting the goals identified in their asset management plans; provided evidence that they are implementing their asset management plans; used real property inventory information and performance measures in decision making; and managed their real property in accordance with their strategic plan, asset management plan, and performance measures. (For more information on the criteria OMB uses to evaluate agencies' efforts, see app. I.)

	4th quarter FY 2004	1st quarter FY 2005	1st quarter FY 2006	1st quarter FY 2007	1st quarter FY 2008	1st quarter FY 2009
GSA	Yellow	Yellow	Green	Green	Green	Green
State	Red	Red	Yellow	Green	Green	Green
VA	Red	Green	Yellow	Green	Green	Green
NASA	Red	Red	Yellow	Green	Yellow	Green
DOE	Red	Red	Yellow	Green	Yellow	Green
Labor	Red	Red	Yellow	Yellow	Yellow	Green
DHHS	Red	Red	Yellow	Yellow	Yellow	Red
DOI	Red	Red	Yellow	Yellow	Red	Red
DOJ	Red	Red	Yellow	Yellow	Green	Green
DOT	Red	Red	Yellow	Yellow	Yellow	Green
USAID[a]	NA	NA	Yellow	Yellow	Yellow	Green
DOD	Red	Red	Yellow	Yellow	Yellow	Red
Army Corps	Red	Red	Red	Yellow	Yellow	Yellow
DHS	Red	Red	Red	Yellow	Yellow	Yellow
USDA	Red	Red	Red	Yellow	Yellow	Yellow

○ Red for unsatisfactory
◐ Yellow for mixed results
● Green for success

Source: OMB scorecards.
Note: USAID was not evaluated until fourth quarter fiscal year 2005.

Figure 1. PMA Executive Branch Management Scorecard Results for the Real Property Initiative.

OMB has also taken some additional steps to improve real property management governmentwide. According to OMB, the federal government disposed of excess real property valued at $1 billion in fiscal year 2008, bringing the total to over $8 billion since fiscal year 2004.[8] OMB also reported success in developing a comprehensive database of federal real property assets, the Federal Real Property Profile (FRPP). OMB recently took further action to improve the reliability of FRPP data by implementing a recommendation we made in April 2007 to develop a framework that agencies can use to better ensure the validity and usefulness of key real property data in the FRPP. According to OMB officials, OMB now requires agency-specific validation and verification plans and has developed a FRPP validation protocol to certify agency data. These actions are positive steps towards eventually developing a database that can be used to improve real property management governmentwide. However, it may take some time for these actions to result in consistently reliable data, and, as described later in this testimony, in recent work we have continued to find problems with the reliability and usefulness of FRPP data.

Furthermore, our work over the past year has found some other positive steps that some agencies have taken to address ongoing challenges. Specifically:

- In September 2008, we found that from fiscal year 2005 through 2007, VA made significant progress in reducing underutilized space (space not used to full capacity) in its buildings from 15.4 million square feet to 5.6 million square feet.[9] We also found that VA's use of various legal authorities, such as its enhanced use lease authority (EUL), which allows it to enter into long-term agreements with public and private entities for the use of VA property in exchange for cash or in-kind consideration, likely contrib uted to its overall reduction of underutilized space since fiscal year 2005. However, our work also shows that VA does not track the overall effect of its use of these authorities or of the space reductions.
- In October 2008, we found that in dealing with repair and maintenance backlogs, six agencies we reviewed focus on maintaining and repairing real property assets that are critical to their missions, and have processe s in place to prioritize maintenance and repair items based on the effects those items may have on their missions.[10]

LONGSTANDING PROBLEMS IN REAL PROPERTY MANAGEMENT PERSIST

In spite of some progress made by OMB and agencies in managing their real property portfolios, our recent work has found that agencies continue to struggle with the long-standing problems that led us to identify federal real property as high-risk: an over-reliance on costly leasing—and challenges GSA faces in its leasing contracting; unreliable data; underutilized and excess property and repair and maintenance backlogs; and ongoing security challenges faced by agencies and, in particular, by the Federal Protective Service (FPS), which is charged with protecting GSA buildings.

Over-Reliance on Costly Leasing Continues, and GSA's Initial Implementation of Leasing Contracting Faced Problems

Over-Reliance on Costly Leasing Continues

One of the major reasons for our designation of federal real property as a high-risk area in January 2003 was the government's overreliance on costly leasing. Under certain conditions, such as fulfilling short-term space needs, leasing may be a lower-cost option than ownership. However, our work over the years has shown that building ownership often costs less than operating leases, especially for long-term space needs.

In January 2008, we reported that federal agencies' extensive reliance on leasing has continued, and that federal agencies occupied about 398 million square feet of leased building space domestically in fiscal year 2006, according to FRPP data.[11] GSA, USPS, and USDA leased about 71 percent of this space, mostly for offices, and the military services leased another 17 percent. For fiscal year 2008, GSA reported that for the first time, it leased more space than it owned.

In 10 GSA and USPS leases that we examined in the January 2008 report, decisions to lease space that would be more cost-effective to own were driven by the limited availability of capital for building ownership and other considerations, such as operational efficiency and security. For example, for four of seven GSA leases we analyzed, leasing was more costly over time than construction—by an estimated $83.3 million over 30 years. Although ownership through construction is often the least expensive option, federal budget scorekeeping rules require the full cost of this option to be recorded up front in the budget, whereas only the annual lease payment and cancellation costs need to be recorded for operating leases, reducing the up-front commitment even though the leases are generally more costly over time. USPS is not subject to the scorekeeping rules and cited operational efficiency and limited capital as its main reasons for leasing.

While OMB made progress in addressing long-standing real property problems, efforts to address the leasing challenge have been limited. We have raised this issue for almost 20 years. Several alternative approaches have been discussed by various stakeholders, including scoring operating leases the same as ownership, but none have been implemented. In our 2008 report, we recommended that OMB, in consultation with the Federal Real Property Council and key stakeholders, develop a strategy to reduce agencies' reliance on leased space for long-term needs when ownership would be less costly. OMB agreed with our recommendation. According to OMB officials, in response to this recommendation, an OMB working group conducted an analysis of lease performance. OMB is currently using this analysis as it works with officials of the new administration to assess overall real property priorities in order to establish a roadmap for further action.

GSA's Initial Implementation of the National Brokers Services Contracts Demonstrated Need for Numerous Improvements

With GSA's ongoing reliance on leasing, it is critical that GSA manage its in-house and contracted leasing activities effectively. However, in January 2007, we identified numerous areas in GSA's implementation of four contracts for national broker services that warranted improvement.[12] Our findings were particularly significant since, over time, GSA expects to outsource the vast majority of its expiring lease workload.

At one time, GSA performed lease acquisition, management, and administration functions entirely in-house. In 1997, however, GSA started entering into contracts for real estate services to carry out a portion of its leasing program, and in October 2004, GSA awarded four contracts to perform broker services nationwide (national broker services), with contract performance beginning on April 1, 2005. GSA awarded two of the four contracts to dual-agency brokerage firms—firms that represent both building owners and tenants (in this case, GSA acting on behalf of a tenant agency). The other two awardees were tenant-only brokerage firms—firms that represent only the tenant in real estate transactions. Because using a dual-agency brokerage firm creates an increased potential for conflicts of interest, federal contracting requirements ordinarily would prohibit federal agencies from using dual-agency brokers, but GSA waived the requirements, as allowed, to increase competition for the leasing contracts.[13] When the contracts were awarded, GSA planned to shift at least 50 percent of its expiring lease workload to the four awardees in the first year of the contracts and to increase their share of GSA's expiring leases to approximately 90 percent by 2010—the fifth and final year of the contracts. As of May 30, 2009, GSA estimated that the total value of the four contracts was $485.6 million.

We reviewed GSA's administration of the four national broker services contracts (i.e., the national broker services program) for the first year of the contracts which ended March 31, 2006. In our January 2007 report, we identified a wide variety of issues related to GSA's early implementation of these contracts. Problems included inadequate controls to (1) prevent conflicts of interest and (2) ensure compliance with federal requirements for safeguarding federal information and information systems used on behalf of

GSA by the four national brokers. We also reported, among other matters, that GSA had not developed a method for quantifying what, if any, savings had resulted from the contracts or for distributing work to the brokers on the basis of their performance, as it had planned. We made 11 recommendations designed to improve GSA's overall management of the national broker services program. As figure 2 shows, GSA has implemented 7 of these 11 recommendations; has taken action to implement another recommendation; and, after consideration, has decided not to implement the remaining 3. (For more details on the issues we reported in January 2007 and GSA's actions to address our recommendations, see app. II). We are encouraged by GSA's actions on our recommendations but have not evaluated their impact.

Category	Recommendation	Status
Conflicts of interest	Assess the adequacy of the two dual-agency brokers' conflict wall controls	●
	Modify the two dual-agency brokers' contracts to ensure that GSA can enforce recommendations resulting from its conflict wall inspections	⊘
	Establish consistent dual-agency and tenant-only conflict-of-interest contract requirements	●
	Establish additional controls to mitigate the inherent conflict of interest created by allowing the brokers to represent the government while negotiating commissions with building owners	⊘
Compliance with Federal Information Security Management Act requirements	Assess the risk from unauthorized access to GSA information collected or maintained by the four brokers	●
	Modify the four brokers' contracts to include controls appropriate to the assessed risk to ensure that the brokers safeguard information in accordance with the Federal Information Security Management Act	⊘
	Test the effectiveness of federal information security policies, procedures, and practices related to the national broker services program	●

(Continued).

Category	Recommendation	Status
Program implementation and evaluation	Develop processes for quantifying expected savings from the national broker services program	●
	To prepare for performance-based distribution, clarify the number and types of completed task orders needed to establish a record of the brokers' performance	◐
	Collect data on GSA's distributions of task orders for rural and urban areas	●
	Clarify and revise terminology in the national broker services program contracts and administrative guide to ensure applicability of evaluation measures and conformance to the National Institutes of Health's performance-related terminology	●

● Recommendation has been implemente

◐ GSA's actions to implement the recommendation are ongoing

⊘ GSA considered but did not implement the recommendationConflicts

Source: GAO.

Figure 2. GSA's Progress in Implementing Our Recommendations on the National Broker Services Program.

Problems with Unreliable Data Persist

Quality governmentwide and agency-specific data are critical for addressing the wide range of problems facing the government in the real property area, including excess and unneeded property, deterioration, and security concerns. In April 2007, we reported that although some agencies have made progress in collecting and reporting standardized real property data for FRPP, data reliability is still a challenge at some of the agencies, and agencies lacked a standard framework for data validation.[14] We are pleased that OMB has implemented our recommendation to develop a framework that agencies can use to better ensure the validity and usefulness of key real property data in the FRPP, as noted earlier. However, in the past 2 years, we have found the following problems with FRPP data:

- In our January 2008 report on agencies' leasing, we found that, while FRPP data were generally reliable for describing the leased inventory, data quality concerns, such as missing data, would limit the usefulness of FRPP for other purposes, such as strategic decision making.[15]
- In our October 2008 report on federal agencies' repair and maintenance backlogs, we found that the way six agencies define and estimate their repair needs or backlogs varies.[16] We also found that, according to OMB officials, FRPP's definition of repair needs was purposefully vague so agencies could use their existing data collection and reporting process. Moreover, we found that condition indexes, which agencies report to FRPP, cannot be compared across agencies because their repair estimates are not comparable. As a result, these condition indexes cannot be used to understand the relative condition or management of agencies' assets. Thus, they should not be used to inform or prioritize funding decisions between agencies. In this report, we recommended that OMB, in consultation with the Federal Accounting Standards Advisory Board, explore the potential for adding a uniform reporting requirement to FRPP to capture the government's fiscal exposure related to real property repair and maintenance. OMB agreed with our recommendation.
- In our February 2009 report on agencies' authorities to retain proceeds from the sale of real property, we found that, because of inconsistent and unreliable reporting, governmentwide data reported to FRPP were not sufficiently reliable to analyze the extent to which the six agencies with authority to sell real property and retain the proceeds from such sales actually sold real property.[17] Such data weaknesses reduce the effectiveness of the FRPP as a tool to enable governmentwide comparisons of real property efforts, such as the effort to reduce the government's portfolio of unneeded property.

Furthermore, although USPS is not required to submit data to FRPP, in December 2007, we found reliability issues with USPS data that also compromised the usefulness of the data for examining USPS's real property performance.[18] Specifically, we found that USPS's Facility Database—developed in 2003 to capture and maintain facility data—has numerous reliability problems and is not used as a centralized source for facility data, in part because of its reliability problems. Moreover, even if the data in the Facility Database were reliable, the database would not help USPS measure facility management performance because it does not track performance indicators nor does it archive data for tracking trends.

Agencies Face Ongoing Challenges with Underutilized Property and Repair and Maintenance Backlogs

In April 2007, we reported that among the problems with real property management that agencies continued to face were excess and underutilized property, deteriorating facilities, and maintenance and repair backlogs. We reported some federal agencies maintain a significant amount of excess and underutilized property. For example, we found that Energy, DHS, and NASA reported that over 10 percent of their facilities were excess or underutilized.[19] Agencies may also underestimate their underutilized property if their data are not reliable. For example, in 2007, we found during limited site visits to USPS facilities that six of the facilities we visited had vacant space that local employees said could be leased, but these facilities were not listed as having vacant, leasable space in USPS's Facilities Database (see fig. 3).[20] At that time, USPS officials acknowledged the vacancies we cited and noted that local officials have few incentives to report facilities' vacant, leasable space in the database.

Underutilized properties present significant potential risks to federal agencies because they are costly to maintain and could be put to more cost-beneficial uses or sold to generate revenue for the government. In 2007, we also reported that addressing the needs of aging and deteriorating federal facilities remains a problem for major real property-holding agencies, and that according to recent estimates, tens of billions of dollars will be needed to repair or restore these assets so that they are fully functional.[21] In October 2008, we reported that agency repair backlog estimates are not comparable and do not accurately capture the government's fiscal exposure.[22] We found that the six agencies we reviewed had different processes in place to periodically assess the condition of their assets and that they also generally used these processes to identify repair and maintenance backlogs for their assets. Five agencies identified repair needs of between $2.3 billion (NASA) and $12 billion (DOI). GSA reported $7 billion in repair needs. The sixth agency, DOD, did not report on its repair needs. Table 1 provides a summary of each agency's estimate of repair needs.

Circle City Station, Indianapolis, Indiana	Denton Main Post Office, Texas	Downtown Finance Station, Gary, Indiana
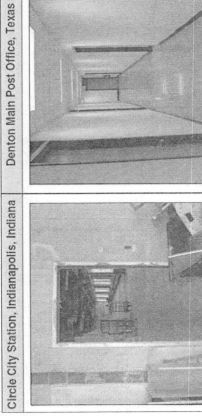		
• **Vacant area:** A large portion of the second floor. • **Status:** Postal officials said the Postal Service never built out the second floor because the space was not needed and could be subleased or returned to building owner. • Status listed in FDB: No vacant leasable space.	• **Vacant area:** Entire second floor of the large post office. • **Status:** Postal officials said half of the building was occupied by other federal agencies that moved out about 10 years ago and that the space could be leased. • Status listed in FDB: No vacant leasable space.	• **Vacant area:** The basement (pictured) is completely vacant, and the second floor is used once per month or less for training. • **Status:** Postal officials said the Postal Service never used more than just the main floor and could lease the excess space. • Status listed in FDB: No vacant leasable space.

Figure 3. (Continued).

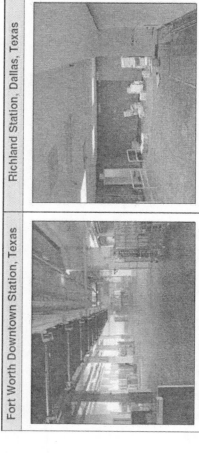

Fort Worth Downtown Station, Texas	Richland Station, Dallas, Texas	East Chicago Main Post Office, Indiana

Fort Worth Downtown Station, Texas

- **Vacant area:** Second floor (pictured) and basement are vacant. Third floor used periodically for storage and training.
- **Status:** Postal officials said most of the building has been vacant since the mail processing function was removed years ago.
- Status listed in FDB: No vacant leasable space.

Richland Station, Dallas, Texas

- **Vacant area:** Much of the second floor of this 53,000-square-foot post office.
- **Status:** Postal officials said the office space has been vacant for years, and another portion (pictured above) has not been occupied since the Postal Service purchased the building in 1989.
- Status listed in FDB: No vacant leasable space.

East Chicago Main Post Office, Indiana

- **Vacant area:** The entire second floor, which consists of several offices.
- **Status:** Postal officials said it has been vacant for years and could be leased.
- Status listed in FDB: No vacant leasable space.

Source: GAO.

Figure 3. Vacant, Possibly Leasable Space in USPS Facilities Not Listed in the Facilities Database (FDB).

Table 1. Selected Agencies' Processes for Conducting Condition Assessments and Estimating Repair Needs to Calculate FRPP Condition Index for Fiscal Year 2007

Dollars in billions

Agency	Assets assessed	Frequency of assessments	What is included in the estimate of repair needs (backlog)	Identified repair needs
DOE	All assets	At least every 5 years	Work not done in time frame identified	$3.3
NASA	All assets	Annually	Work required to bring the asset up to current standards	2.3
DOI	Assets valued at $5,000 or more	Every 5 years	Work not done in time frame identified	12.0[a]
VA	All assets	At least every 3 years	Work required to correct identified deficiencies in systems determined to be in	5.9
GSA	All assets	Every 2 years	Work identified to be done now or within the next 10 years	7.0
DOD	All assets	Varies by military service	No backlog estimated	b

Source: GAO analysis.

[a] According to DOI officials, DOI recognizes that due to the scope, nature and variety of DOI assets, exact estimates of backlogs are very difficult to determine. As a result, DOI prefers to think of its estimate as a range.

[b] DOD did not compute a dollar amount for repair needs in 2007.

Agencies and Federal Protective Service Face Ongoing Security Challenges

In addition to other ongoing real property management challenges, the threat of terrorism has increased the emphasis on physical security for federal real property assets. In 2007, we reported that all nine major real property-holding agencies reported using risk-based approaches to prioritize security needs, as we have suggested, but cited a lack of resources for security enhancements as an ongoing problem. For example, according to GSA officials, obtaining funding for security countermeasures, both security fixtures and equipment, is a challenge not only within GSA but for GSA's tenant agencies as well.[23]

Moreover, last week we testified before the Senate Committee on Homeland Security and Governmental Affairs that preliminary results show that the Federal Protective Service's (FPS) ability to protect federal facilities is hampered by weaknesses in its contract security guard program.[24] We found that FPS does not fully ensure that its contract security guards have the training and certifications required to be deployed to a federal facility and has limited assurance that its guards are complying with post orders. For example, FPS does not have specific national guidance on when and how guard inspections should be performed; and FPS's inspections of guard posts at federal facilities are inconsistent, and the quality varied in the six regions we visited. Moreover, we identified substantial security vulnerabilities related to FPS's guard program. GAO investigators carrying the components for an improvised explosive device successfully passed undetected through security checkpoints monitored by FPS's guards at each of the 10 level IV federal facilities where we conducted covert testing.[25] Once GAO investigators passed the control access points, they assembled the explosive device and walked freely around several floors of these level IV facilities with the device in a briefcase. In response to our briefing on these findings, FPS has recently taken some actions including increasing the frequency of intrusion testing and guard inspections. However, implementing these changes may be challenging, according to FPS. We previously testified before this subcommittee in 2008 that FPS faces operational challenges, funding challenges, and limitations with performance measures to assess the effectiveness of its efforts to protect federal facilities. We recommended, among other things, that the Secretary of DHS direct the Director of FPS to develop and implement a strategic approach to better manage its staffing resources, evaluate current and alternative funding mechanisms, and develop appropriate performance measures. DHS agreed with the recommendations. According to FPS officials, FPS is working on implementing these recommendations.[26]

UNDERLYING OBSTACLES HAMPER AGENCIES' REAL PROPERTY REFORM EFFORTS GOVERNMENTWIDE

As GAO has reported in the past, real property management problems have been exacerbated by deep-rooted obstacles that include competing stakeholder interests, various legal and budget-related limitations, and weaknesses in agencies' capital planning. While reforms to date are positive, the new administration and Congress will be challenged to sustain reform momentum and reach consensus on how the obstacles should be addressed.

Several Agencies Cited Competing Stakeholder Interests as Impeding Real Property Management Decision Making

In 2007, we found that some major real property-holding agencies reported that competing local, state, and political interests often impede their ability to make real property management decisions, such as decisions about disposing of unneeded property and acquiring real property. For example, we found that USPS was no longer pursuing a 2002 goal of reducing the number of "redundant, low-value" retail facilities, in part, because of legal restrictions on and political pressures against closing them.[27] To close a post office, USPS is required to, among other things, formally announce its intention to close the facility, analyze the impact of the closure on the community, and solicit comments from the community. Similarly, VA officials reported that disposal is often not an option for most properties because of political stakeholders and constituencies, including historic building advocates or local communities that want to maintain their relationship with VA. In addition, Interior officials reported that the department faces significant challenges in balancing the needs and concerns of local and state governments, historical preservation offices, political interests, and others, particularly when coupled with budget constraints.[28] If the interests of competing stakeholders are not appropriately addressed early in the planning stage, they can adversely affect the cost, schedule and scope of a project.

Despite its significance, the obstacle of competing stakeholder interests has gone unaddressed in the real property initiative. It is important to note that there is precedent for lessening the impact of competing stakeholder interests. Base Realignment and Closure Act (BRAC) decisions, by design, are intended to be removed from the political process, and Congress approves all BRAC decisions as a whole. OMB staff said they recognize the significance of the obstacle and told us that FRPC would begin to address the issue after the inventory is established and other reforms are initiated. But until this issue is addressed, less than optimal decisions based on factors other than what is best for the government as a whole may continue.

Legal and Budgetary Limitations Continue to Hamper Agencies' Disposal Efforts

As discussed earlier, budgetary limitations that hinder agencies' ability to fund ownership leads agencies to rely on costly leased space to meet new space needs. Furthermore, the administrative complexity and costs of disposing of federal property continue to hamper efforts by some agencies to address their excess and underutilized real property problems. Federal agencies are required by law to assess and pay for any environmental cleanup that may be needed before disposing of a property—a process that may require years of study and result in significant costs. As valuable as these legal requirements are, their administrative complexity and the associated costs of complying with them create disincentives to the disposal of excess property. For example, we reported that VA, like all federal agencies, must comply with federal laws and regulations governing property disposal that are intended to protect subsequent users of the property from environmental hazards and to preserve historically significant sites, among other purposes.[29] We have reported that some VA managers have retained excess property because the administrative complexity and costs of complying with these requirements were disincentives to disposal.[30] Additionally, some agencies reported that the costs of cleanup and demolition sometimes exceed the costs of continuing to maintain a property that has been shut down. In such cases, in the short run, it can be more beneficial economically to retain the asset in a shutdown status.

Some federal agencies have been granted authorities to enter into EULs or to retain proceeds from the sale of real property. Recently, in February 2009, we reported that the 10 largest real property-holding agencies have different authorities for entering into EULs and retaining proceeds from the sale of real property, including whether the agency can use any retained proceeds without further congressional action such as an annual appropriation act, as shown in table 2.[31]

Officials at five of the six agencies with the authority to retain proceeds from the sale of real property, (the Forest Service, GSA, State, USPS, and VA) said this authority is a strong incentive to sell real property.[32] Officials at the five agencies that do not have the authority to retain proceeds from the sale of real property (DOE; DOI; DOJ; NASA; and USDA except for the Forest Service) said they would like to have such expanded authorities to help manage their real property portfolios. However, officials at two of those agencies said that, because of challenges such as the security needs or remote locations of most of their properties, it was unlikely that they would sell many properties.

Table 2. Agencies' Authorities Regarding EULs and Real Property Sales

Agency	Authority to enter into EULs and retain leasing proceeds	Authority to use proceeds from EULs without further congressional action	Authority to sell real property and retain sales proceeds	Authority to use proceeds from sales without further congressional action
DOD	X	X	X	X[a]
DOE	X[b]			
GSA	X		X	
DOI[c]				
DOJ				
NASA	X	X		
State[d]	X	X	X	X[e]
USDA (except the Agricultural Research Service[f]and the Forest Service)				
USDA (Forest Service)[g]	X[h]	X	X	X
USPS	X	X	X	X
VA	X	X	X	[i]

Source: GAO analysis and information provided by the above agencies.

Note: Authorities through fiscal year 2008.

[a] n certain cases, the use of proceeds from the sale of DOD real property is subject to further congressional action.

[b] According to DOE, the department has determined that it has EUL authority on the basis of the definition set forth in OMB Circular A-11 (June 2008). DOE officials said that the department has not entered into any EULs using this authority.

[c] While DOI has certain authorities to sell real property, we did not include in the scope of our review lands managed by DOI.

^d State has used its authority under 22 U.S.C. § 300 to exchange, lease, or license real property outside of the country. According to State, in exceptional cases, the department has relied on this authority to enter into long-term leases to conserve historically significant properties, such as the Talleyrand Building in Paris, France. State's authorization to sell and retain proceeds from the sale of real property applies to its properties located outside of the United States and to properties located within the United States acquired for an exchange with a specified foreign government.

^e According to State, committee reports accompanying State's appropriations acts routinely require the department to notify Congress through the reprogramming process of the specific planned use of the proceeds of the sale of excess property. Furthermore, State indicated that it routinely includes discussion of the use of proceeds from the sale of real property in its budget justifications and financial plans.

^f Because USDA's Agricultural Research Service received pilot authority to enter into EULs for certain properties effective June 2008, but had not entered into any EULs during our review, we did not include it in the scope of our review.

^g We are listing the Forest Service separately from USDA because it has authority to sell administrative property and retain the proceeds from the sales, unlike the rest of USDA.

^h Although the Forest Service has EUL authority, it has not used that authority.

^I Under certain circumstances, VA can use the proceeds from the sale of former EUL property without further congressional action.

We have previously found that, for agencies which are required to fund the costs of preparing property for disposal, the inability to retain any of the proceeds acts as an additional disincentive to disposing of real property. As we have testified previously, it seems reasonable to allow agencies to retain enough of the proceeds to recoup the costs of disposal, and it may make sense to permit agencies to retain additional proceeds for reinvestment in real property where a need exists.[33] However, in considering whether to allow federal agencies to retain proceeds from real property transactions, it is important for Congress to ensure that it maintains appropriate control and oversight over these funds, including the ability to redistribute the funds to accommodate changing needs.

Two current initiatives relate to these issues. The administration's 2010 budget includes a real property legislative proposal that, among other things, would permit agencies to retain the net proceeds from the transfer or sale of real property subject to further Congressional action. On May 19, 2009, H.R. 2495, the Federal Real Property Disposal Enhancement Act of 2009, was introduced in the House of Representatives, and this bill, like the administration's legislative proposal, would authorize federal agencies to retain net proceeds from the transfer or sale of real property subject to further congressional action. Additionally, both the administration's legislative proposal and H.R. 2497 would establish a pilot program for the expedited disposal of federal real property.

Weaknesses in Capital Planning Still Exists

Over the years, we have reported that prudent capital planning can help agencies to make the most of limited resources, and failure to make timely and effective capital acquisitions can result in acquisitions that cost more than anticipated, fall behind schedule, and fail to meet mission needs and goals. In addition, Congress and OMB have acknowledged the need to improve federal decision making in the area of capital investment. A number of laws enacted in the 1990s placed increased emphasis on improving capital decision-making practices and *OMB's Capital Programming Guide* and its revisions to *Circular A-11* have attempted to address the government's shortcomings in this area. However, we have continued to find limitations in OMB's efforts to improve capital planning governmentwide. For example, real property is one of the major types of capital assets that agencies acquire, and therefore shortcomings in the capital planning and decision-making area have clear implications for the administration's real property initiative.[34] However, while OMB staff said that agency asset management plans are supposed to align with their capital plans, OMB does not assess whether the plans are aligned. Moreover, we found that guidance for the asset management plans does not discuss how these plans should be linked with agencies' broader capital planning efforts outlined in the *Capital Programming Guide*. Without a clear linkage or crosswalk between the guidance for the two documents, agencies may not link them. Furthermore, the relationship between real property goals specified in the asset management plans and longer-term capital plans may not be clear. In April 2007, we recommended that OMB, in conjunction with the FRPC, should establish a clearer link between agencies' efforts under the real property initiative and broader capital planning guidance.[35] According to OMB officials, OMB is currently considering options to strengthen agencies' application of the capital planning process as part of *Circular A-11*, with a focus on preventing cost overruns and schedule delays.

Federal Real Property Reform Efforts Continue to Face Challenges

In 2007, we concluded that the executive order on real property management and the addition of real property to PMA provided a good foundation for strategically managing federal real property and addressing long-standing problems. These efforts directly addressed the concerns we had raised in past high-risk reports about the lack of a governmentwide focus on real property management problems and generally constitute what we envisioned as a transformation strategy for this area. However, we found that these efforts were in the early stages of implementation, and the problems that led to our high-risk designation—excess property, repair backlogs, data issues, reliance on costly leasing, and security challenges— still existed. As a result, this area remains high risk until agencies show significant results in eliminating the problems by, for example, reducing inventories of excess facilities and making headway in addressing the repair backlog. While the prior administration took several steps to overcome some obstacles in the real property area, the obstacles posed by competing local, state, and political interests went largely unaddressed, and the linkage between the real property initiative and broader agency capital planning efforts is not clear. In 2007, we recommended that OMB, in conjunction with the FRPC, develop an action plan for how the FRPC will address these key problems.[36] According to OMB officials, these key problems are among those being considered as OMB works with administration officials to assess overall real property priorities in order to establish a roadmap for further action. While reforms to date are positive, the new administration and Congress will be challenged to sustain reform momentum and reach consensus on how the ongoing obstacles should be addressed.

Madam Chair, this concludes my prepared statement. I would be happy to respond to any questions you or other Members of the Subcommittee may have at this time.

Green standards ●	Yellow standards ◐	Red standards ○
Agency: • Meets all yellow standards for success; • Established an OMB-approved 3-year rolling timeline with date certain deadlines by which agency will address opportunities and determine its priorities as identified in the asset management plan; • Demonstrated steps taken toward implementation of asset management plan as stated in yellow standards (including meeting established deadlines in 3-year timeline, meeting prioritized management improvement actions, maintaining appropriate amount of holdings, and estimating and optimizing cost levels); • Accurate and current asset inventory information and asset maximization performance measures are used routinely in management decision making (such as reducing the amount of unneeded and underused properties); and • The management of agency property assets is consistent with the agency's overall strategic plan, the agency asset management plan, and the performance measures established by the FRPC as stated in the Federal Real Property Asset Management Executive Order.	Agency: • Has a Senior Real Property Officer (SRPO) who actively serves on the FRPC; • Established asset management performance measures, consistent with the published requirements of the FRPC ∴ Completed and maintained a comprehensive inventory and profile of agency real property, consistent with the published requirements of the FRPC; • Provided timely and accurate information for inclusion into the governmentwide real property inventory database; and • Developed an OMB-approved comprehensive asset management plan that: • Complies with guidance established by the FRPC • Includes policies and methodologies for maintaining property holdings in an amount and type according to agency budget and mission • Seeks to optimize level of real property operating, maintenance, and security costs.	Agency: • Does not actively participate on the FRPC; • Has not established asset management performance measures or has asset management performance measures that are inconsistent with the published requirements of the FRPC; • Has not completed or does not maintain a comprehensive inventory and profile of agency real property consistent with the published requirements of the FRPC; • Does not provide timely and accurate information for inclusion into the governmentwide real property inventory database; or • Has not developed an OMB-approved comprehensive asset management plan.

Source: OMB.

Figure 1. PMA Executive Branch Management Scorecard Standards for the Real Property Initiative.

APPENDIX I: EXECUTIVE BRANCH MANAGEMENT SCORECARD STANDARDS FOR THE REAL PROPERTY INITIATIVE

In April 2007, we found that adding real property asset management to the President's Management Agenda (PMA) had increased its visibility as a key management challenge and focused greater attention on real property issues across the government. As part of this effort, the Office of Management and Budget (OMB) identified goals for agencies to achieve in right-sizing their real property portfolios. To achieve these goals and gauge an agency's success in accurately accounting for, maintaining, and managing its real property assets so as to efficiently meet its goals and objectives, the administration established the real property scorecard in the third quarter of fiscal year 2004. The scorecard consists of 13 standards that agencies must meet to achieve the highest status—green— as shown in figure 1. These 13 standards include 8 standards needed to achieve yellow status, plus 5 additional standards. An agency reaches green or yellow status if it meets all of the standards for success listed in the corresponding column in figure 1 and red status if it has any of the shortcomings listed in the column for red standards.

APPENDIX II: STATUS GAO RECOMMENDATIONS RELATED TO GSA'S NATIONAL BROKER SERVICES PROGRAM

Table 1. Explanation and Implementation Status of Recommendations Related to GSA's National Broker Services Program

Reported issue	Recommendation	Status/Actions taken
1. While the General Services Administration (GSA) had confirmed that the two dual agency firms (firms that represent both building owners and tenants) had established "conflict walls" to help prevent the electronic and physical sharing of information between the brokers' employees, it had not assessed whether the conflict walls were adequate to prevent unauthorized information sharing between employees within the same firm who represent GSA, and other employees within the same firm who represent building owners.	Assess the adequacy of the two dual-agencies' conflict wall controls and recommend actions, if applicable, to correct any identified weaknesses.	Implemented GSA assessed the adequacy of the dual agencies' conflict walls and, on May 22, 2007, concluded that the conflict walls were satisfactory.

Table 1. (Continued).

Reported issue	Recommendation	Status/Actions taken
2. GSA conducted a preliminary inspection of the conflict walls maintained by the two dual-agency brokers, but had not ensured that the brokers implemented its inspection recommendations. GSA's inaction was attributable, in part, to uncertainty about whether GSA's contracts with the brokers permitted it to require brokers to implement its inspection recommendations.	Modify the two dual-agency contracts to ensure that GSA can enforce recommendations resulting from its conflict wall inspections.	Not implemented GSA reviewed its contracts with the two dual-agency brokers and determined that the language in the contracts was already sufficient to ensure that it could enforce compliance with its inspection recommendations. Therefore, according to GSA, there was no need to modify the contracts.
3. GSA had not established consistent conflict-of-interest contract requirements for all of its contractors. Specifically, while GSA required its dual-agency brokers (firms that represent both building owners and tenants) to (1) execute additional agreements to safeguard proprietary information; (2) notify GSA of any conflicts of interest discovered during the performance of work; and (3) include a conflict-of-interest clause in all of their subcontracts, its contracts with the two tenant-only contractors (firms that represent only tenants) did not contain similar requirements.	Establish consistent dual-agency and tenant-only conflict-of-interest contract requirements, including, at a minimum, the three conflict-of-interest requirements that address situations also faced by the two tenant-only firms.	Implemented GSA included the three conflict of interest requirements in its contracts with the two tenant-only brokers in May 2007. In addition, GSA included other conflict-of-interest requirements in the tenant-only broker contracts in response to other questions we posed during our review. Previously these requirements had been only explicitly applicable to the dual-agency brokers. Ensuring consistency in contractor requirements will help ensure that tenant-only firms are aware of all of the requirements applicable to their disclosure of potential or actual conflicts of interest. GSA also revised its administrative guide to reflect this point.

Reported issue	Recommendation	Status/Actions taken
4. Despite federal requirements, GSA had not fully assessed the risk and magnitude of harm that could result from the misuse of information and information systems used on behalf of GSA by the four national brokers. Such an assessment is required by the Federal Information Security Management Act to help ensure that contractors and others are protecting an agency's information and information systems in a manner commensurate with the risk level assigned to the information and information systems by the agency.	Assess the risk and magnitude of harm that could result from unauthorized access to, or use, disclosure, disruption, modification, or destruction of, GSA information collected or maintained by the four brokers (and their subcontractors) and the information systems used by the brokers on behalf of GSA.	Implemented GSA performed the recommended risk assessment on August 30, 2007, and concluded that the risk level was "moderate."
5. While requirements of the Federal Information Security Management Act are applicable to the national broker services brokers, GSA's contracts with them did not require the brokers to comply with the act's requirements.	Modify the four national broker services' contracts to include controls appropriate to the assessed risk to ensure that the brokers and their subcontractors safeguard information and information systems in accordance with the Federal Information Security Management Act.	Not implemented GSA informed us in August 2007 that it had developed a plan to complete the assessment and accreditation required to bring each of the four brokers into compliance with the Federal Information Security Management Act. As part of that process, GSA determined that it was in the best interest of the government to identify and analyze

Table 1. (Continued).

Reported issue	Recommendation	Status/Actions taken
		the brokers' existing controls and use them, where possible, to meet the requirements of the act. GSA expected this process would take severalmonths to complete. In the interim, GSA stated that it would be inappropriate to modify the contracts. However, GSA further stated that, if warranted by its assessments of the brokers, it may modify its individual contracts with the brokers in the future.
6. Despite federal requirements, GSA had not tested the information security controls associated with its national brokers program, including the controls used by its four national brokers. The Federal Information Security Management Act requires such testing to ensure that controls are adequate for protecting agency information, including information maintained by contractors (and subcontractors). Testing must be conducted at least once per year.	Test the effectiveness of federal information security policies, procedures, and practices related to the national broker services program, including, as appropriate, broker controls for safeguarding GSA's information.	Implemented GSA developed a process to test the effectiveness of controls used for safeguarding its program information and, as of March 15, 2008, had completed testing at one of the four brokers. According to GSA, "The continuous monitoring required by its process means that it is never complete but must be done repeatedly..." throughout the life of the contracts.

Reported issue	Recommendation	Status/Actions taken
7. Conflict of interest controls were not adequate to ensure that brokers would not increase the government's rental costs by favoring building owners who offer them higher commissions. Specifically, we concluded that, until such time as GSA establishes effective controls to mitigate the brokers' inherent conflict of interest by, among other possible actions, precluding them from accepting commissions in excess of the rate approved by the contracting officer's technical representatives and included in GSA's solicitation for offers, there will remain at least the perception that the brokers might favor–at the government's expense—building owners who pay higher commissions.	Establish additional controls to mitigate the inherent conflict of interest created by allowing the brokers to represent the government, while also negotiating their commissions with building owners.	Not implemented

GSA initiated a "multi-faceted approach" to address this recommendation, including an assessment of (1) peer review findings and (2) the results of prior protests on leasing actions. According to GSA, its assessment did not identify any instances of abuse or inappropriate actions by the brokers. Consequently, GSA determined that there was no need to establish additionalcontrols. |
| 8. While GSA anticipated that using national brokers would results in (1) reduce rental costs to the government, and (2) agency savings from reduced fees, administrative expenses, and personnel by shifting costs to the national broker services contracts, it had not developed a process for quantifying the expected savings. | Develop processes for quantifying expected savings from (1) rent reductions attributable to the brokers' greater knowledge of the commercial real estate market and (2) agency savings associated with reduced fees, administration expenses, personnel costs, and operational efficiencies associated with using the national broker services contracts. | Implemented

GSA developed a process for quantifyingsavings from the national broker servicesprogram. Specifically, GSA extracted "as much relevant and reliable historical dataaas available" on its prior (regional/zonal) contracts and compared the data to available data on the national broker services contracts |

Table 1. (Continued).

Reported issue	Recommendation	Status/Actions taken
		through the end of the first quarter of fiscal year 2008. GSA's analysis identified numerous cost savings attributable to its use of the national broker services contracts, including $25 million in commission credits earned by the brokers and/or credited to customer agencies.
9. While GSA initially expected to start performance-based task order distributions after the first year of the contract, it delayed doing so because too few task orders had been completed to establish a record of their performance on a variety of commission-eligible task orders. When we completed our review in January 2007, GSA expected to begin performance-based distributions on April 1, 2007—the start of the third contract year. Before GSA can move to performance-based distributions, we reported that GSA must (1) ensure that it has sufficient data on each broker's performance and (2) develop clearly defined guidance and processes for allocating additional future work to those brokers who excel relative to the others.	As part of GSA's effort to prepare for performance-based distribution decisions, clarify the number and types of completed task orders needed to establish a record of the brokers' performance.	Open[a] According to a GSA official, GSA developed and tentatively approved a plan for implementing performance-based work distributions. However, it was forced to suspend implementation of the plan when testing revealed unspecified flaws that would have negatively impacted the national broker services program. According to this official, GSA is now focusing its efforts on developing a methodology for implementing performance-based work distributions for the follow-on national broker services contracts that are expected to begin on April 1, 2010.

Reported issue	Recommendation	Status/Actions taken
10. Although GSA collected data on the number and size of the task orders distributed to the four national broker services brokers, it did not collect data on the geographic area (e.g., rural or urban) covered by the task orders. Such data was needed because GSA's contracts with the brokers specify that each broker will be provided projects on a nationwide basis in both rural and urban areas during the initial period of contract performance, as long as their performance is acceptable.	Begin collecting data on GSA's distributions of task orders for rural and urban areas (i.e., similar geographic areas) during the initial period of the contracts.	Implemented GSA developed a methodology and subsequently collected and analyzed data to better inform its distribution of task orders between the brokers during the initial period of the contracts.
11. The national contracts and administrative guidance had numerous inaccuracies, inconsistencies, and omissions that raised questions about how GSA could ensure consistency in its regions' evaluations of the brokers' performance. Problems included inapplicable evaluation criteria; variations in the criteria identified for use at different evaluation stages by the contracts, and inconsistencies between GSA's and National Institutes of Health's (NIH) performance-related terminology.	To improve overall management of the national broker services program, (1) clarify the national broker services contracts and the administrative guide to ensure that the evaluation measures used are applicable to the brokers' performance at each stage of evaluation. (2) Regarding the brokers' required annual performance evaluations, revise the terminology in GSA's contracts and administrative guide, as appropriate, to conform to NIH's required evaluation factors.	Open, but implementedb GSA revised its administrative guide to clarify when each evaluation factor is to be used in assessing contractor performance at each stage of evaluation. The revised guidance also (1) clarifies how the National Institutes of Health's required annual evaluation fits within GSA's evaluation processes and

Table 1. (Continued).

Reported issue	Recommendation	Status/Actions taken
	(3) In addition, ensure that the various evaluation stages and processes are properly and adequately described in GSA's administrative guide.	(2) describes GSA's various evaluation stages and processes. (GAO intends to initiate action to close this recommendation.)

Source: GAO.

[a] In describing the status of recommendation 9 as "open", we are referring to the formal status of this recommendation in our recommendation tracking system. The description of GSA's ongoing actions demonstrates that GSA's actions to implement the recommendation are ongoing, as summarized in Figure 2 of the testimony.

[b] In describing the status of recommendation 11 as "open, but implemented" we are referring to the fact that in our recommendation tracking system, the recommendation is currently listed as open. However, as the description of GSA's actions to implement the recommendation demonstrate, we believe GSA has adequately implemented this recommendation and we plan to close this recommendation as implemented in our tracking system.

End Notes

[1] GAO, *High-Risk Series: Federal Real Property*, GAO-03-122 (Washington, D.C.; Jan. 2003); the report on real property is a companion to GAO's 2003 high-risk update, GAO, *High-Risk Series: An Update*, GAO-03-119 (Washington, D.C.; Jan. 2003); GAO, *High-Risk Series: An Update*, GAO-05-207 (Washington, D.C.; Jan. 2005), and GAO, *High-Risk Series: An Update*, GAO-07-310 (Washington, D.C.; Jan. 2007.)

[2] GAO *High-Risk Series: An Update*, GAO-09-271 (Washington, D.C.: January 2009).

[3] See, among others referenced in this testimony, GAO, *Federal Real Property: Progress Made Toward Addressing Problems, but Underlying Obstacles Continue to Hamper Reform*, GAO-07-349, (Washington, D.C., Apr. 13, 2007) and GAO, *Federal Real Property: An Update on High-Risk Issues*, GAO-07-895T, (Washington, D.C. May 24, 2007).

[4] Appendix, *The President's Budget Request for Fiscal Year 2010*, General Provisions Government-Wide, p. 14-16, and *The Federal Real Property Disposal Enhancement Act of 2009*, H.R. 2495, 111th Cong. (2009).

[5] Our 2007 report and testimony focusing on federal real property as high risk (GAO-07-349 and GAO-07-895T) from which we drew much of this testimony, focused on eight of the largest real property-holding agencies, including the Departments of Defense (DOD), Energy (DOE), Homeland Security (DHS), the Interior (DOI), State (State); and Veterans Affairs (VA); GSA; and the National Aeronautics and Space Administration (NASA). Also included is the United States Postal Service (USPS), which is an independent establishment in the executive branch and is among the largest property holders in terms of owned and leased space. Other recent work has included different agencies, which are described in the relevant sections of this testimony.

[6] Executive Order 13327 was signed by the President in February 2004 and established new federal property guidelines for 24 executive branch departments and agencies, not including USPS. The PMA is an administration program that has raised the visibility of key governmentwide management challenges, among other things. The real property PMA initiative, formally called the Federal Asset Management Initiative, is a program initiative applicable to the 15 largest landholding agencies.

[7] The agencies included on OMB's quarterly scorecard include GSA, State, VA, NASA, DOE, the Department of Labor (Labor), the Department of Health and Human Services (DHHS), the Department of Justice (DOJ), the Department of Transportation (DOT), the United States Agency for International Development (USAID), DOD, Army Corps of Engineers (Army Corps), DHS, and the United States Department of Agriculture (USDA).

[8] The source for real property disposal valuation is the FRPP. The FRPP calculates total disposals by using the market price for those properties disposed through sale and the replacement value for those properties disposed through demolition or other conveyance. The replacement value represents the cost necessary to replace a facility and is often a higher than market value.

[9] GAO, *Federal Real Property: Progress Made in Reducing Unneeded Property, but VA Needs Better Information to Make Further Reductions*, GAO-08-939 (Washington, D.C.: Sept. 10, 2008).

[10] GAO, *Federal Real Property: Government's Fiscal Exposure from Repair and Maintenance Backlogs Is Unclear*, GAO-09-10 (Washington, D.C.: Oct. 16, 2008). For this report, we reviewed the six agencies that had told us in 2007 they had over $1 billion in repair and maintenance backlogs associated with their held assets: DOD, DOE, DOI, VA, GSA, and NASA.

[11] GAO, *Federal Real Property: Strategy Needed to Address Agencies' Long-standing Reliance on Costly Leasing*, GAO-08-197, (Washington, D.C.: Jan 24, 2008).

[12] GAO, *GSA Leasing: Initial Implementation of the National Broker Services Contracts Demonstrates Need for Improvements*, GAO-07-17, (Washington, D.C.: Jan. 31, 2007).

[13] While GSA waived the contracting requirements, it developed controls to help detect and mitigate conflicts of interest, including a control requiring the two dual-agency brokers to develop and maintain "conflict walls" to isolate GSA's procurement-sensitive information.

[14] GAO-07-349.

[15] GAO-08-197

[16] GAO-09-10. The six agencies reviewed in this study each had told us in 2007 that they had over $1 billion in repair and maintenance backlogs and included DOD, DOE, DOI, VA, GSA, State, and NASA.

[17] GAO, *Federal Real Property: Authorities and Actions Regarding Enhanced Use Leases and Sale of Unneeded Real Property*, GAO-09-283R (Washington, D.C.: Feb. 17, 2009). The six agencies with authority to sell real property and retain the proceeds from such sales are DOD, GSA, The United States Department of Agriculture's (USDA) Forest Service, USPS, and VA.

[18] GAO, *U.S. Postal Service Facilities: Improvements in Data Would Strengthen Maintenance and Alignment of Access to Retail Services*, GAO-08-41, (Washington, D.C.: Dec. 10, 2007).

[19] GAO-07-349.

[20] GAO-08-41

[21] GAO-07-349.

[22] GAO-09-10. The six agencies reviewed in this study—DOD, DOE, DOI, VA, GSA, and NASA—each had told us in 2007 that they had over $1 billion in repair and maintenance backlogs.

[23] GAO-07-349.

[24] GAO, Homeland Security: Preliminary Results Show Federal Protective Service's Ability to Protect Federal Facilities Is Hampered By Weaknesses in Its Contract Security Guard Program. GAO-09-859T. (Washington, D.C.: July 8, 2009). FPS, which is part of DHS, provides law enforcement and related security functions to about 9,000 GSA facilities. To accomplish its mission of protecting GSA facilities, in 2009, FPS had a budget of about $1 billion, 1,200 full-time employees, and about 13,000 contract security guards.

[25] Of the 10 level IV facilities we penetrated, 8 were government owned, 2 were leased, and included offices of a U.S. Senator and U.S. Representative, as well as agencies such as the DOH, State, and DOJ. The level of security FPS provides at each of the 9,000 facilities varies depending on the building's security level. Based on DOJ's 1995 Vulnerability Assessment Guidelines, there are five types of security levels, with a level IV facility—which includes high risk law enforcement and intelligence agencies—having over 450 employees and a high volume of public contact. FPS does not have responsibility for a Level V facility, which includes the White House and the Central Intelligence Agency. The Interagency Security Committee has recently promulgated new security level standards that will supersede the 1995 DOJ standards.

[26] GAO, *Homeland Security: The Federal Protective Service Faces Several Challenges That Hamper Its Ability to Protect Federal Facilities*, GAO-08-683, (Washington, D.C.: June 11, 2008) and GAO, *Homeland Security: The Federal Protective Service Faces Several Challenges That Raise Concerns About Protection of Federal Facilities*, GAO-08-897T, (Washington, D.C.: June 19, 2008.)

[27] GAO-08-41.

[28] GAO-07-349.

[29] GAO, *VA Health Care: Key Challenges to Aligning Capital Assets and Enhancing Veterans' Care*, GAO-05-429 (Washington, D.C.: Aug. 5, 2005).

[30] GAO-05-429.

[31] GAO-09-283R. For this review, we studied the authorities of the 10 largest real property-holding federal agencies (by value of real property). These 10 agencies include USDA, DOD, DOE, DOI, DOJ, State, VA, GSA, NASA, and USPS. For the purposes of this review, the term "real property" does not include real property that DOD has or is planning to dispose of through the Base Realignment and Closure Act (BRAC) process, lands managed by DOI or the Forest Service (except for Forest Service administrative sites), and transfers of individual properties specifically authorized by Congress. Under the BRAC process, the Secretary of Defense is authorized to close certain military bases and dispose of property. In the scope of our review, we included real property disposed of by DOD through its authority to convey or lease existing property and facilities outside of the BRAC process.

[32] The sixth agency, DOD, stated that this authority was not a strong incentive to dispose of excess real property.

[33] GAO-07-895T.

[34] Other capital assets include information technology, major equipment, and intellectual property.

[35] GAO-07-349.

[36] GAO-07-349.

In: Federal Real Property Disposition   ISBN: 978-1-62100-048-8
Editor: Iain D. Haque   © 2012 Nova Science Publishers, Inc.

Chapter 5

FEDERAL REAL PROPERTY: AUTHORITIES AND ACTIONS REGARDING ENHANCED USE LEASES AND SALE OF UNNEEDED REAL PROPERTY[*]

United States Government Accountability Office

Many federal agencies hold real property that they do not need, including property that is underutilized or excess.[1] Such properties present significant potential risks to federal agencies because they are costly to maintain and could be put to more cost-beneficial uses or sold to generate revenue for the government. We first designated federal real property management as a high-risk area in January 2003 due to longstanding problems with underutilized and excess property, among other things.[2] After our high-risk designation, President George W. Bush added real property management to the President's Management Agenda and directed that the Federal Real Property Profile (FRPP) be established as a comprehensive database of real property under the control and custody of executive branch agencies, with agencies required to report on their real property assets each year.[3] The President also established a goal of disposing of $15 billion in unneeded real property assets by 2015 to encourage agencies to right-size their portfolios by eliminating unneeded property.

---

[*] This is an edited, reformatted and augmented version of the United States Government Accountability Office publication GAO-09-283R, dated February 17, 2009.

Some federal agencies have been granted authorities to enter into enhanced use leases (EUL)—typically long-term agreements with public and private entities for the use of federal property, resulting in cash and/or in-kind consideration for the agency—or to retain the proceeds from the sale of real property. Given the large number of unneeded properties being held by the federal government, you asked that we review how agencies are using their disposal authorities. Therefore, we addressed (1) what authorities the 10 largest real property holding agencies have to enter into EULs and retain proceeds from the sale of real property; (2) the extent to which agencies with authority to retain proceeds sold real property and how they have used the proceeds; and (3) the relationship, if any, between agencies having the authority to enter into EULs or retain sales proceeds and the amount of real property that they retained or sold.

To address these questions, we analyzed agencies' legal authorities related to EULs and the sale and retention of proceeds of real property; analyzed agency real property and FRPP data; and gathered, analyzed, and synthesized documentary and testimonial evidence of the 10 largest real property holding federal agencies (by value of real property). These 10 agencies include the Department of Agriculture (USDA), Department of Defense (DOD), Department of Energy (DOE), Department of the Interior (DOI), Department of Justice (DOJ), Department of State (State),

Department of Veterans Affairs (VA), General Services Administration (GSA), National Aeronautics and Space Administration (NASA), and the United States Postal Service (USPS). For the purposes of this review, the term "real property" does not include real property that DOD has or is planning to dispose of through the Base Realignment and Closure Act (BRAC) process,[4] lands managed by DOI or the Forest Service (except for Forest Service administrative sites), and transfers of individual properties specifically authorized by Congress. We also conducted site visits of real property that agencies have recently sold, exchanged, or were attempting to sell, and a property being leased under an EUL agreement and collected data from agencies on their real property sales during fiscal years 2006 and 2007. (See encl. I for additional information on our scope and methodology.)

We conducted our work in Arlington, Va.; Camp Verde, Ariz.; Colorado Springs, Colo.; Denver; Estes Park, Colo.; Glendale, Ariz.; Guilderland, N.Y.; Hillsborough, N.J.; Loveland, Colo.; Middle River, Md.; New York City; Peoria, Ariz.; Rotterdam, N.Y.; Scotia, N.Y.; Scottsdale, Ariz.; Sedona, Ariz.; Tucson, Ariz.; and Washington, D.C., from April 2008 through February 2009.

RESULTS IN BRIEF

The 10 largest real property holding agencies have different authorities regarding EULs and retention of proceeds from the sale of real property. As of the end of fiscal year 2008,

- six agencies had both the authority to enter into EULs and sell and retain the proceeds from the sale of real property (DOD, GSA, State, USDA's Forest Service, USPS, and VA);
- two agencies had EUL authority but no authority to retain proceeds from the sale of real property (DOE and NASA); and
- three agencies had no authority either to enter into EULs or retain proceeds from the sale of real property (USDA,[5] excluding the Forest Service; DOI;[6] and DOJ).

Authorities are agency-specific and include different provisions. For example, while VA is authorized to enter into EULs for "underutilized" or "unutilized" real property, DOD is authorized to enter into EULs only for "nonexcess" real property. In addition, while DOD, GSA, and VA have the authority to retain proceeds from the sale of real property, DOD (in some cases), GSA, and VA are required to follow several steps before possibly selling the property, including offering it to other federal agencies, eligible organizations that will use the property to assist the homeless, and other public benefit purposes. However, the Forest Service, State, and USPS sell real property and retain the proceeds without following these additional steps. Moreover, four agencies have the authority to retain proceeds from the sale of real property and use them without further congressional action (DOD in certain cases, the Forest Service, State,[7] and USPS) while further congressional action is required before two agencies (VA for nonEUL property[8] and GSA) may use the proceeds.

The six agencies with authority to retain proceeds reported selling property to varying extents and using proceeds primarily to help manage their real property portfolios. Governmentwide data reported to the FRPP were not sufficiently reliable to quantify the extent to which these agencies sold real property. As a result, we were unable to use the FRPP to analyze the number of sales of real property by agencies with the authority to retain proceeds. However, the six agencies we contacted that have authority to retain proceeds from the sale of real property provided data on their net proceeds from the sale of real property during fiscal years 2006 and 2007, which ranged from $21 million to \$541 million per agency. While some properties sold for tens of thousands of dollars, others sold for over \$200 million. Agencies generally reported using the sales proceeds to manage their real property portfolios, such as rental of space, building operations, new construction and acquisition, maintenance, and repairs and operations.

Agency officials generally said that the authorities to enter into EULs and sell real property and retain the proceeds influenced the amount of property that is kept and sold and that they preferred using the authorities that were the least restrictive. Because we were unable to quantify the number of properties that agencies sold during fiscal years 2006 and 2007, we asked agency officials about their views on the relationship between having the authorities to enter into EULs or retain sales proceeds and the amount of real property that they sell. Of the six agencies with the authority to retain proceeds from the sale of real property, officials at five agencies (the Forest Service, GSA, State, USPS, and VA) said that this authority is a strong incentive to sell real property, while officials at DOD said that the authority to retain proceeds is not a strong incentive to sell real property. Agencies with both authorities—to enter into EULs and retain proceeds from the sale of real property— prefer using the authority with the fewest restrictions. For example, VA indicated that EUL authority allows the agency to manage unneeded property because (1) VA may enter into EUL agreements without following steps required to sell real property, such as screening the property for use by the homeless, and (2) VA has the authority to retain and spend proceeds generated from EULs without the need for further congressional action. On the other hand, officials at USPS said that USPS has little incentive to enter into EULs and instead focuses on selling or exchanging property to maximize benefits to its real estate portfolio. The five agencies that do not have the authority to retain proceeds from the sale of real property (DOE; DOI; DOJ; NASA; and USDA except for the Forest Service), provided mixed responses about the extent to which such an authority would be an incentive to sell unneeded real property. While officials at all five agencies said that they would like to have such expanded authorities to help manage their real property portfolios, officials at two of those agencies said that due to challenges such as the security needs or remote locations of most of their properties, it was unlikely that they would sell many properties.

We requested comments on a draft of this report from the 10 real property holding agencies in our review and OMB. DOE, GSA, and DOI agreed with the information presented in the report. DOE, GSA, NASA, OMB, State, USDA, and VA provided technical clarifications, which we incorporated throughout the report as appropriate. The other agencies did not provide comments.

Table 1. Agencies' Authorities Regarding EULs and Real Property Sales

Agency	Authority to enter into EULs and retain leasing proceeds	Authority to use proceeds from EULs without further congressional action	Authority to sell real property and retain sales proceeds	Authority to use proceeds from sales without further congressional action
DOD	X	X	X	Xa
DOE	Xb			
GSA	X		X	
DOIc				
DOJ				
NASA	X	X		
Stated	X	X	X	Xe
USDA (except the Agricultural Research Servicef and the Forest Service)				
USDA (Forest Service)g	Xh	X	X	X
USPS	X	X	X	X
VA	X	X	X	i

Source: GAO analysis and information provided by the above agencies. Note: Authorities through fiscal year 2008.

[a] In certain cases, the use of proceeds from the sale of DOD real property is subject to further congressional action. See footnote 13.

[b] According to DOE, the department has determined that it has EUL authority on the basis of the definition set forth in OMB Circular A-11 (June 2008). DOE officials said that the department has not entered into any EULs using this authority.

[c] While DOI has certain authorities to sell real property, we did not include in the scope of our review lands managed by DOI.

[d] State has used its authority under 22 U.S.C. § 300 to exchange, lease, or license real property outside of the country. According to State, in exceptional cases, the department has relied on this authority to enter into long-term leases to conserve historically significant properties, such as the Talleyrand Building in Paris, France. State's authorization to sell and retain proceeds from the sale of real property applies to its properties located outside of the United States and to

properties located within the United States acquired for an exchange with a specified foreign government.

e According to State, committee reports accompanying State's appropriations acts routinely require the department to notify Congress through the reprogramming process of the specific planned use of the proceeds of the sale of excess property. Furthermore, State indicated that it routinely includes discussion of the use of proceeds from the sale of real property in its budget justifications and financial plans.

f Because USDA's Agricultural Research Service received pilot authority to enter into EULs for certain properties effective June 2008, but had not entered into any EULs during our review, we did not include it in the scope of our review.

g We are listing the Forest Service separately from USDA because it has authority to sell administrative property and retain the proceeds from the sales, unlike the rest of USDA.

h Although the Forest Service has EUL authority, it has not used that authority.

i Under certain circumstances, VA can use the proceeds from the sale of former EUL property without further congressional action. See footnote 8.

AGENCIES HAVE DIFFERENT AUTHORITIES REGARDING EULS AND RETENTION OF PROCEEDS FROM SALE OF REAL PROPERTY

Separate legislation has provided agencies with their own statutory authorities regarding EULs and retaining proceeds from the sale of real property. The 10 largest real property holding agencies have different authorities for EULs and retention of proceeds from the sale of real property. As of the end of fiscal year 2008, eight agencies had the authority to enter into EULs (DOD, DOE, GSA, NASA, State, USDA's Forest Service, USPS, and VA) and six agencies (DOD, the Forest Service, GSA, State, USPS, and VA) had the authority to sell and retain proceeds from the sale of real property. Six agencies had both authorities to enter into EULs and to retain proceeds from the sale of real property (DOD, GSA, State, USDA's Forest Service, USPS, and VA); two agencies had EUL authority but no authority to retain proceeds from the sale of real property (DOE and NASA); and three agencies had no authority to enter into EULs or retain proceeds from the sale of real property (USDA, excluding the Forest Service; DOI; and DOJ).[9] The authorities of these agencies are shown in table 1. For more information on agencies' legal authorities related to real property EULs, sales, and retention of proceeds, see enclosure II.

Authorities are agency-specific and include different provisions. For example, while VA is authorized to enter into EULs for "underutilized" or "unutilized" real property, DOD is authorized to enter into EULs only for "nonexcess" real property.[10] In addition, some agencies must follow the requirements in Title 40 of the United States Code and the McKinney-Vento Homeless Assistance Act before selling real property—and some of these steps may result in the property being disposed of with no proceeds—while other agencies' authorities exempt them from following these requirements.[11] Congress enacted the McKinney-Vento Homeless Assistance Act as a comprehensive federal response to homelessness and enacted the public benefit conveyance (PBC) program as one means of disposing of surplus federal property, whereby state or local governments and certain tax-exempt nonprofit organizations can obtain surplus real property for public uses, such as public heath or educational facilities and public parks and recreational areas. GSA and VA, for example, have the authority to retain proceeds from the sale of real property but must, before offering property for sale, follow the requirements under Title 40 of the United States Code and the McKinney-Vento Homeless Assistance Act. Although DOD also has authority to retain the proceeds from the sale of real property, in certain cases, the department is exempt from following the requirements under Title 40 relating to real property disposition and the McKinney Act.[12] Furthermore, four agencies with the authority to retain proceeds from the sale of real property (DOD, in certain cases;[13] the Forest Service; State; and USPS) have authority to use these proceeds without further congressional action, while two agencies with authority to retain proceeds from the sale of real property, (VA for nonEUL property and GSA) require further congressional action before using them. Figure 1 shows the steps that GSA must follow to sell excess real property and retain the proceeds. (Encl. III illustrates the steps each agency must follow to sell real property.)

By contrast, the Forest Service, State, and USPS do not follow the requirements[14] under Title 40 of the United States Code and the McKinney-Vento Homeless Assistance Act when they wish to sell real property, both reducing the time and effort involved and eliminating instances in which the agency disposes of the property at a discount of up to 100 percent of fair market value. For example, figure 2 shows the steps that State must follow to sell overseas real property.

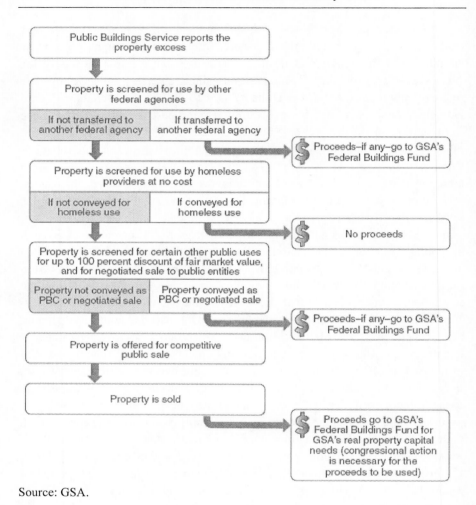

Source: GSA.

Figure 1. GSA's Process for Selling Excess GSA-Controlled Real Property.

How these proceeds can be spent also varies, as described fully in enclosure II. Table 2 provides a summary of the steps that agencies must follow when selling real property and retaining proceeds.

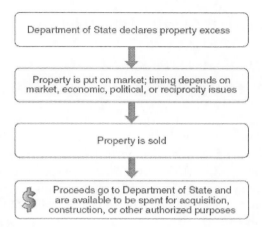

Source: State Department.

Figure 2. State Department's Process for Selling Excess Real Property Located Outside of the United States.

Table 2. Summary of Major Steps that Agencies Follow to Sell Real Property

Agency	Property declared excess	Screened for use by other agencies	Screened for use by homeless	Screened for public benefit use
DOD[a]	Yes	Yes	Yes	Yes
DOD[b,c]	No	No	No	No
GSA	Yes	Yes	Yes	Yes
State	Yes	No	No	No
USDA/Forest Service (for administrative sites)	No	No	No	No
USPS	Yes	No	No	No
VA	Yes	Yes	Yes	Yes

Source: GAO analysis; information provided by the above agencies.

Note: The agencies listed in this table are only those with the authority to retain proceeds from the sale of real property. See enclosure II for the specific authorities provided in this table.

[a] 40 U.S.C. § 572. Under this authority, while the Administrator of GSA is authorized to dispose of DOD property, DOD is the recipient of the proceeds.

[b] 10 U.S.C. § 2854a.

[c] 10 U.S.C. § 2878.

AGENCIES WITH AUTHORITY TO RETAIN PROCEEDS FROM SALE OF REAL PROPERTY REPORTED SELLING PROPERTY TO VARYING EXTENTS AND USING PROCEEDS FOR PROPERTY MANAGEMENT

Governmentwide data reported to the FRPP were not sufficiently reliable to analyze the extent to which the six agencies with authority to retain proceeds sold real property, due to inconsistent and unreliable reporting. However, these six agencies (DOD, the Forest Service, GSA, State, USPS, and VA) reported selling property to varying extents, with net proceeds ranging from $21 million to $541 million during fiscal years 2006 and 2007. In addition, five agencies (DOD, GSA, State, the Forest Service, and VA) reported using sales proceeds to manage their real property portfolios, such as rental of space, building operations, new construction and acquisition, maintenance, and repairs and alterations, while USPS reported depositing the proceeds into its general fund.

FRPP Data on Real Property Disposal Were Unreliable

According to GSA officials, a data element on disposition (which includes disposition by sale as well as other methods) was added to the FRPP as of fiscal year 2006 to identify unneeded assets that have been removed from the FRPP inventory and to track the volume of disposals to support the strategic goal of right-sizing the federal real property inventory. However, we found inconsistent and unreliable reporting within the disposal data element on the method of disposal and were therefore unable to use the FRPP to analyze the number of sales of real property by agencies with the authority to retain proceeds. For example, the Air Force reported that in fiscal year 2006, it disposed of 4,397 assets by sale, as well as disposing of a number of assets by demolition, federal transfer, or other means. In fiscal year 2007, however, it reported disposing of 12,423 assets, all in the "other" category.[15] Because all of its disposed assets were reported in the "other" category for fiscal year 2007, unlike in the prior fiscal year, we asked Air Force officials about the reasonableness of the data. Air Force officials agreed that the disposal method data summarized and reported in 2007 did not provide disposal information comparable to the level of detail provided in 2006. They said that the primary cause for insufficient data detail has been resolved and that they plan to provide better data in future reporting that more accurately reflects disposal methods.

GSA officials said that every time a new data element is added to the FRPP, the data for that element are likely to be less reliable because agencies need to learn the process and determine how to provide these data. GSA reviews the data submitted by federal agencies and notifies the relevant agencies of any inconsistencies and anomalies. If an agency does not address the inconsistencies or anomalies, GSA will report these to OMB; OMB takes these into account when rating the agencies on their real property management initiative efforts. Nevertheless, these data weaknesses reduce the effectiveness of the FRPP as a tool to enable governmentwide comparisons of real property efforts, such as the effort to reduce the government's portfolio of unneeded property.

Agencies with Authority to Retain Proceeds Reported Selling Real Property to Varying Extent

While we were unable to analyze the governmentwide FRPP database to determine the number of properties sold by agencies with authority to retain proceeds,[16] we asked the six agencies that have authority to retain proceeds from the sale of real property to provide information on the net proceeds received during fiscal years 2006 and 2007. As shown in Table 3, the sales proceeds received by individual agencies in our review ranged from $21 million to $541 million during those 2 years. The highest level of net proceeds for these 2 years was reported by State, largely due to the sale of a facility known as the Navy Annex in London for $494 million.

Of the six agencies with the authority to sell real property and retain the proceeds, two (State and USPS) use in-house staff to handle the sales, while the other three agencies use GSA for some or all of their sales. Under the Federal Management Regulation, landholding agencies must report excess real property to GSA, which is generally responsible for disposing of real property unless an agency has specific or delegated authority to do so.[17] Property sales handled by GSA are typically sold through auctions. We found that agencies with the authority to retain proceeds from the sale of real property had sold a variety of types of properties in the past several years (see fig. 3).

Table 3. Real Property Sales Proceeds during Fiscal Year 2006 and Fiscal Year 2007, by Agency

Agency	FY 2006 proceeds	FY 2007 proceeds	FY 2006 and FY 2007 total proceeds
DOD	$14,070,949	$41,787,312	$55,858,261
GSA	52,049,163	82,218,326	134,267,489
State	36,035,010	505,145,944	541,180,954
USDA-Forest Service	12,600,000	8,700,000	21,300,000
USPS	91,367,745	201,753,000	293,120,745
VA[a]	22,319,702	0	22,319,702

Sources: DOD, GSA, State, USDA, USPS, and VA.

[a] VA reported that it did not sell any properties through its Capital Asset Fund authority, which authorizes it to sell real property and retain the proceeds, but that it sold one property, shown in this table. The property, the Lakeside VA Medical Center in Chicago, was sold under an EUL agreement after determining that it was no longer needed by the agency. VA's proceeds from the sale of the Lakeside VA Medical Center were $50 million, which included a net present value rental return of $28 million received in 2005 for a 75-year EUL term and an additional $22 million received in 2006, reflected in this table, with the actual closing of the sale of the property.

Former Army housing in Rotterdam, New York

Figure 3. (Continued).

Former Forest Service property, Camp Verde, Arizona

Former federal building in Colorado Springs, Colorado

Figure 3. (Continued).

State Department's former Navy Annex in London, England

Sources : GAO (Army Rotterdam housing, Forest Service Camp Verde, and Colorado Springs federal building); Department of State (London Navy Annex).

Figure 3. Examples of Recently Sold Properties by Agencies with Authority to Retain Proceeds.

The sales prices for these recently sold properties varied considerably. While some properties sold for tens of thousands of dollars, one sold for nearly $500 million. Information provided by agency officials on the above properties included the following:

- State's London, England, Navy Annex building sold in 2007 for $494 million, when the London real estate market was at its peak. State Department officials said the sale of this building, which was owned by State but previously used by the Navy, was unique because the sales proceeds from the Navy Annex will be used to build a new embassy in London, rather than used to fund worldwide priorities. State officials provided information on two other examples of sales that they said were more typical, involving the sales of former marine security guard quarters in Cape Town, South Africa, and Quito, Ecuador, in 2008, for $1.1 million and $1.8 million, respectively. The proceeds from those sales were deposited into the department's asset management account to be used for worldwide priorities.

- The Army sold a former Army housing complex in Rotterdam, N.Y., for $1.8 million in 2008. The Army determined this property was excess because it had more housing in the area than it needed to serve its mission. The property, which included several apartment and other buildings on about 8 acres of land, was sold through GSA's online auction for slightly over its appraised value.
- The Forest Service sold two of four parcels of administrative land it offered for sale through GSA's online auction at Camp Verde, Ariz. The first parcel consisted of about 1.6 acres of unimproved land in a residential neighborhood that was sold to private citizens in 2006 for $155,000. The second parcel consisted of about 119 acres of mostly unimproved land that was sold to the town of Camp Verde in 2008 for $2.4 million. The other two parcels did not sell—a fact that Forest Service officials attributed to a downturn in the real estate market.
- GSA sold a federal building in Colorado Springs, Colo., for $890,000 in 2009. The property consisted of about 1.7 acres of land and a 2-story brick office building built in 1962. Formerly leased to the Air Force, the building had been vacant since December 2007. The property was sold through GSA's online auction.

Agencies Reported Using Sales Proceeds Mainly for Real Property Portfolio Management Purposes

Agencies reported using sale proceeds mainly to help manage their real property portfolios. (Encl. II states how agencies are authorized to use proceeds.) For example, a Forest Service official said that the Forest Service used the proceeds from the Camp Verde sale described above to build a new ranger station at Camp Verde. GSA indicated that its sales proceeds are deposited into GSA's Federal Buildings Fund and used for real property management purposes, such as rental of space, building operations, new construction and acquisition, and repairs and alterations. State Department officials said that the proceeds are collected centrally and used for priorities established by the department's Bureau of Overseas Buildings Operations, including purchasing housing and other properties, constructing new facilities, or rehabilitating existing facilities. USPS officials said that the agency deposits its proceeds from the sale of real property into its general fund, where they become part of USPS's funds for use for agency priorities.

AUTHORITIES AFFECT HOW AGENCIES MANAGE THEIR REAL PROPERTY PORTFOLIO

Agency officials generally said that the authorities to enter into EULs and sell and retain sales proceeds influenced the amount of property that is sold and that they preferred using the authorities that were the least restrictive. The five agencies that do not have the authority to retain proceeds from the sale of real property (DOE; DOI; DOJ; NASA; and USDA, except for the Forest Service), indicated that they would favor having this authority to help manage their real property.

Agencies with Authority for Both EUL and Retention of Sales Proceeds Preferred the Authority Seen as Less Restrictive or More Advantageous

We asked agency officials for their views on the relationship between having the authorities to enter into EULs or to sell real property and retain the sales proceeds and the amount of real property that they sell. Of the six agencies with the authority to retain the proceeds from the sale of real property, officials at five agencies (the Forest Service, GSA, State, USPS, and VA) said that this authority is a strong incentive to sell real property, while officials at one agency, DOD, which had the authority to enter into EULs without offering the properties to the homeless and other federal agencies—said that the authority to retain proceeds is not a strong incentive to sell real property. Officials from five agencies that had authorities to enter into EULs and to retain the proceeds from the sale of real property—GSA, DOD, USDA's Forest Service, USPS, and VA—all stated preferences for the authority seen as less restrictive or more financially advantageous to the agency.[18] State, which also has the authority to enter into EULS and retain the proceeds from the sale of real property, indicated that retaining sales proceeds is the more critical part of its program, but also foresees increasing opportunities for EULs in the future.

DOD and VA officials said that because EULs provide greater incentives, the agencies place greater emphasis on entering into EULs, compared to real property sales. DOD officials emphasized the potential of EULs to serve the department's mission, while stating that its authority to retain proceeds from the sale of real property was not a strong incentive to sell unneeded real property. For example, headquarters DOD officials said that there was little emphasis or potential at DOD for selling excess real property outside of the BRAC process, in part because that process was the department's major initiative to consolidate its real property and had largely taken care of the opportunity to dispose of DOD real property. Disincentives to selling real property, according to DOD officials, include the length of time it can take, since such property must first be offered to other federal agencies, the homeless, and other public benefit uses, and the fact that much DOD property cannot be sold to a private entity for security reasons.

In contrast, DOD officials emphasized the potential for EULs to maximize the utility and value of its real property and to serve its mission needs, and each service has a Web site focused on its existing and proposed EULs. In prior work, we found that EULs are a land use planning tool for DOD that Army and Air Force are using to gain in-kind services.[19] DOD is authorized to enter into EULs only for nonexcess property, and officials made the distinction between DOD's authority to enter into EULs for nonexcess property and its authority to sell and retain proceeds from the sale of excess real property. However, it was not always clear how DOD determined whether properties were suitable for EULs. For example, Army officials said that the Army considers EULs for properties it would not consider excess because the property creates a buffer zone or security perimeter for an installation. However, the Army entered into a long-term EUL agreement for a mixed-used development of hotel and retail space at Redstone Arsenal, Ala., on Army property that lies outside of the installation's fence and gate. Army officials said that they see the use as compatible with a buffer zone and wanted to maintain some control over the property because a training site is nearby.

Similarly, Air Force officials said that unutilized property may be nonexcess but suitable for an EUL because it is needed for a buffer zone or to avoid encroachment. However, it has proposed a long-term EUL agreement for a hotel/resort development at Emerald Breeze, on 17 acres of Air Force property on an island off the coast of Florida that is not directly adjacent to an installation. Air Force officials said that every EUL agreement states that the lease can be terminated at any time for a national emergency. This allows the Air Force more flexibility than excessing and selling the property, at which point it would lose the right to reacquire it during a national emergency. In addition, an Air Force official said that under the terms of excessing real property, no property is declared excess until a determination has been made that it is excess. Therefore, until that determination is made, the Air Force does not consider that property excess, and it may consider an EUL for that property.

According to VA officials, VA places greater emphasis on entering into EULs, compared to real property sales, in part because VA can enter into EULs with fewer restrictions than under its Capital Asset Fund (CAF) authority to sell and retain proceeds of real property.[20] For example, VA can enter into an EUL without first screening the property for homeless use, as it must for property it wishes to sell under its CAF authority. Moreover, VA has the authority to retain and spend proceeds from EULs without the need for further congressional action, while proceeds retained under CAF authority are subject to further congressional action. [21] In addition, VA is authorized to use EUL proceeds for purposes unrelated to real property, such as providing health care services, which are not permitted under VA's CAF authority. VA officials said that in addition, EULs allow VA to realign its asset portfolio in a way that supports its mission by using EULs to obtain facilities, services, in-kind consideration, or revenue for VA requirements that would otherwise be unavailable or unaffordable. The officials added that local and state government, veterans groups, private partners, and nonprofit entities and other community members potentially benefit when these properties are redeveloped to provide new services and economic opportunities to veterans and the community. VA produces an annual report that discusses and tracks the benefits of its active EULs for the past fiscal year.

VA officials said that although they believe retaining proceeds from the sale of real property is a strong incentive, other factors, such as the needs of veterans' service organizations and the community that are complimentary to VA's mission, are of equal importance. This review and past work found that VA has used authorities, such as EULs, to provide services for veterans, such as homeless housing, drug rehabilitation, and childcare, and to generate revenue. For example, in 2006, at Fort Howard, Md., VA entered into an EUL to use nearly 300,000 square feet of vacant space to develop a retirement community, with priority placement for veterans. Conversely, in another EUL, VA is leasing property in Hillsborough, N.J., called Veterans Industrial Park to a company that subleases the property to a variety of commercial interests needing warehouse or light manufacturing space, as well as the county government. VA officials said that VA did not consider selling this property because, in 1999, when the agency entered into the EUL agreement, it did not have the authority to retain the proceeds from the sale of real property. In addition, GSA had a similar property nearby that the agency had been unable to sell. Other than a small area on the property that is used for VA services to collect and distribute military clothing to homeless veterans, the property lessees are commercial renters who are not providing any direct services to VA. However, VA officials said that it considers such EULs to be in the agency's interest, as VA is receiving about $300,000 to $390,000 a year from rental income that it can use for the agency's priorities.[22] (See fig. 4 for photographs of this property.)

Source: GAO.

Figure 4. Veterans Industrial Park, Which Is Generating Lease Payments to VA.

GSA stated that while it has the authority to enter into EULs and sell and retain the proceeds from real property sales, it believes that budget scorekeeping rules under OMB Circular A-11 limit the agency's ability to maximize usage of its EUL authority. In contrast, GSA officials said that the agency's ability to retain proceeds is a strong incentive to dispose of excess real property.[23] From fiscal years 2002 to 2007, it reported 271 assets as excess, helping to avoid more than $600 million of repair and alterations liability and providing GSA with almost $140 million of proceeds, which GSA uses as reinvestment funds for its portfolio of core assets. GSA officials said that it is unlikely that sales proceeds have been seen as an offset to the following year's appropriation. According to GSA officials, the agency's sale of a 1.9 million square-foot facility known as the Middle River Depot in Baltimore County, Md., is a good illustration of how retention of proceeds can motivate GSA to dispose of excess real property and obtain the best value for the government from its real property sales.

Source: GAO.

Figure 5. Middle River Depot, Md., Sold by GSA in 2006.

The Middle River Depot, a large warehouse used to build B-26 bombers in World War II, with some associated buildings and land, sold for $37.5 million in 2006. In this case, GSA decided there was no government need for the property, and Congress passed legislation in 2004 for GSA to sell this property and keep the proceeds.[24] The main challenges in marketing and selling the property were community concerns and the state's insistence that the warehouse be covered by a historic easement.[25] GSA officials said that GSA expended considerable time and effort into overcoming these challenges, such as negotiating with the Maryland Historical Trust until it came to an understanding of the basic alterations that would and would not be permitted to the building. GSA subsequently provided this information to prospective bidders. GSA officials said that the agency was motivated to sell the property at the highest possible price because GSA was authorized to retain the proceeds (see fig. 5).

Officials at USPS, which has authority to enter into EULs and sell real property and retain proceeds, said that the Postal Service prefers to sell or exchange unneeded property. Officials said that USPS's authority provides the agency with a strong incentive to actively sell or exchange underutilized property that has a high value. Because of the relatively streamlined process to sell real property, compared to other agencies, and its ability to retain and use sales proceeds for any USPS purpose without further congressional action, it has little incentive to enter into EULs and rarely does so. Three former USPS properties that were sold or exchanged in the past few years were initiated by other parties wanting to purchase the building or land. For example, the state of New York approached USPS in the 1990s about purchasing the Farley Building in Manhattan, a historic, 1.4 million-square-foot building across the street from Pennsylvania Station (see fig. 6) to redevelop the building into a new train station to be named the Moynihan Station. USPS sold the Farley Building in 2007 and is in the process of consolidating its operations into two other existing buildings and 250,000 square feet of leaseback space in the Farley building. According to USPS officials, the sale of the Farley building generated financial proceeds to USPS,[26] reduced deferred maintenance costs, consolidated USPS operations into less space overall, and resulted in reduced operating costs. In the other two cases, in Denver and Scottsdale, Ariz., USPS exchanged old post offices with various parties (the city of Denver and a health care company) that sought the postal property and financed new post offices. In both cases, according to USPS's analysis, USPS benefited financially from the transaction, as well as gaining modern and more efficient facilities in return for older ones.

Source: GAO.

Figure 6. Farley Building in New York City, Sold by USPS in 2007.

State Department officials also told us that the authority to retain proceeds is an incentive to dispose of excess real property because it allows the agency to direct resources from the sale of real property to other pressing facilities needs. Although further congressional action is not needed before State may use proceeds from the sales of real property, the department notifies Congress about its intended use of the proceeds in its budget justifications and financial plans.

Officials at the Forest Service, which has authorities to enter into EULs and retain proceeds from the sale of real property, said that the agency's authority to retain proceeds is a strong incentive to sell real property. Officials at this agency described active efforts to analyze their portfolios to find opportunities to sell unneeded real property. Forest Service officials said that since it received authority to retain proceeds in 2001, it has disposed of more properties than before it had the authority.[27] The Forest Service officials said that the agency has benefited in two primary ways from this authority. First, the Forest Service has used proceeds to help address a large backlog of deferred maintenance needs. Second, because it may use proceeds to construct new ranger stations, they said this authority has helped the Forest Service realign its infrastructure to better meet its current mission. Forest Service officials said that a major reason that the authority to keep the proceeds has functioned as an incentive is that the Forest Service's policy is to use proceeds for local or regional priorities where the property is sold. A Forest Service site in Sedona, Ariz., illustrates these benefits. The Forest Service sold a property that had been used as a ranger station, along with some related buildings and land, for $8.4 million to build a new ranger station on another site (see fig. 7).

The previous Forest Service ranger station had significant deferred maintenance needs and was on a side street with little traffic in the town of Sedona. According to a Forest Service official, since the new ranger station opened along the main highway to Sedona in April 2008, average monthly visits by the public to the ranger station have increased significantly.

Source: GAO.

Figure 7. New Forest Service Ranger Station in Sedona, Ariz., Funded by Sale of Another Property.

The Forest Service has also sold properties with lower real estate values, including one in Estes Park, Colo., that was sold in August 2008 for $440,000. According to a Forest Service official, the Forest Service no longer ran an office out of Estes Park and did not need the property. In addition, the property had significant maintenance needs. Forest Service officials said that the biggest challenge regarding the sale of this property was the downturn in the housing market, and that the agency faces a similar challenge in selling many other properties under such economic conditions. Even so, the Forest Service considers the disposition a success because it no longer has to maintain this unneeded property and plans to use the proceeds for high-priority deferred maintenance needs.

Agencies without Authority to Retain Proceeds from Real Property Sales Provided Mixed Responses on whether Such Authority Would Be a Strong Incentive

Officials at the five agencies we contacted that do not have the authority to retain proceeds from the sale of real property (DOE; DOI; DOJ; NASA; and USDA, except for the Forest Service) provided mixed responses when asked about the extent to which such an authority would be an incentive to sell more real property. Officials at the five agencies said their agencies would like to have expanded authorities with which to manage their real property portfolio, including the authority to enter into EULs and retain the proceeds from the sale of real property. However, officials at two of those agencies said that due to challenges such as the security needs or remote locations of most of their properties, it was unlikely there would be a significant number of real properties that were appropriate to sell.

One challenge that agencies face in disposing of real properties is maintaining them until they can be sold. We visited a former USDA Agricultural Research Service laboratory in Phoenix that was for sale. The laboratory was vacated in January 2006 when the staff moved to another location. During our visit, we observed that property had been vandalized and copper from the buildings and part of a greenhouse had been stolen. While GSA is marketing and attempting to sell the property, USDA remains responsible for maintaining it until May 1, 2009, before responsibility is transferred to GSA under certain conditions.

Vandalized USDA laboratory

Destroyed greenhouse

Source: GAO.

Figure 8. Former USDA Laboratory for Sale in Phoenix.

Agencies may also face challenges in exercising their EUL authority. NASA, one agency that does not have the authority to retain proceeds from the sale of real property, has had the authority to enter into EULs at two centers; as of December 31, 2008, a new agencywide authority gives NASA the ability to enter into EULs. In recent work, we found that while NASA has realized some EUL-related financial benefits, among other things—most of which would not have been realized by NASA without this authority—the agency did not have adequate controls in place to ensure accountability and transparency and to protect the government.[28] NASA accepted our recommendations and developed agencywide policy for the administration of EULs and for the financial management of the revenue derived from EULs.[29] NASA officials said that they use EULs, rather than selling the property, when the agency believes the property may be needed in the future or wants to maintain some control over the property.

ENCLOSURE I: SCOPE AND METHODOLOGY

Our objective was to review how agencies are using their disposal authorities. To accomplish this, we addressed (1) what authorities the 10 largest real property holding agencies have to enter into enhanced use leases (EUL) or retain proceeds from the sale of real property; (2) the extent to which agencies with authority to retain proceeds sold real property and how they have used the proceeds; and (3) the relationship, if any, between agencies having the authority to enter into EULs or retain sales proceeds and the amount of real property that they retained or sold.

To determine what authorities the 10 largest real property holding agencies have regarding EULs and retention of proceeds from the sale of real property, we first identified the 10 agencies that reported holding real property with the highest values to the Federal Real Property Profile (FRPP) in fiscal year 2007. These 10 agencies include the Department of Agriculture (USDA), Department of Defense (DOD), Department of Energy (DOE), Department of the Interior (DOI), Department of Justice (DOJ), Department of State (State), Department of Veterans Affairs (VA), General Services Administration (GSA), National Aeronautics and Space Administration (NASA), and the United States Postal Service (USPS). For the purposes of this review, the term "real property" does not include real property that DOD has or is planning to dispose of through the Base Realignment and Closure Act (BRAC) process,[30] lands managed by DOI or the Forest Service (except for Forest Service administrative sites), and transfers of individual properties specifically authorized by Congress. We then conducted legal research and interviewed officials at those 10 agencies regarding their authorities to enter into EULs and sell and retain the proceeds from the sales of real property. We also reviewed agencies' asset management plans and real property management policies on issues involving excessing properties, selling properties, and entering into EULs. In addition, we reviewed GSA guidance for federal agencies on declaring excess and selling real property. Furthermore, we reviewed prior GAO reports on real property management, leasing, and selling federal real property.

To determine to what extent agencies with authority to retain proceeds sold real property and how they have used the proceeds, we first obtained and analyzed real property disposition data from the FRPP regarding the 10 agencies. We also interviewed officials from the Office of Management and Budget (OMB) about the reliability of the disposition information contained in the FRPP. After we determined that the FRPP disposition data were unreliable for our purposes, we obtained information on the amount of proceeds from the sales of real property received during fiscal years 2006 and 2007 from the six agencies that are authorized to retain proceeds. We did not independently validate the accuracy of the sales proceeds information that the agencies provided because we considered the data to be sufficiently reliable for our purposes, which was focused more on whether the agencies sold any real property and what they used the proceeds for, rather than an accurate accounting of the funds received for those properties. In addition, we interviewed officials from the 10 agencies about the processes that they follow in disposing of real property and their recent real property sales, including the reasons for selling the properties, how they were marketed, and the challenges faced.

To determine the relationship, if any, between agencies having the authority to enter into EULs or retain sales proceeds and the amount of real property that they retained or sold, we interviewed agency officials about the factors they considered in deciding whether or how to dispose of unneeded real property, including the authorities available. We also visited a VA EUL site in Hillsborough, N.J., and interviewed officials from the property management and leasing companies about the agreement and how the property was being used.

To help address the second and third research questions, we also visited federal properties that had been sold or were for sale in Camp Verde, Ariz.; Colorado Springs, Colo.; Denver; Estes Park, Colo.; Glendale, Ariz.;

Guilderland, N.Y.; Loveland, Colo.; Middle River, Md.; New York; Peoria, Ariz., Rotterdam, N.Y.; Scotia, N.Y.; Scottsdale, Ariz.; Sedona, Ariz.; and Tucson, Ariz. During the site visits, we interviewed officials involved in the sales, including officials from the agencies that held the properties; GSA; and, when available, the buyers. We also obtained information from the agencies that were authorized to retain the sales proceeds on how they used the proceeds.

ENCLOSURE II: SELECTED REAL PROPERTY AUTHORITIES AND RETENTION OF PROCEEDS AUTHORITIES FOR MAJOR REAL PROPERTY HOLDING AGENCIES

Real property holding agency	Authority	Description of authority
DOD[a]	Leases of Non-Excess Property of Military Departments 10 U.S.C. § 2667	The Secretary of a military department is authorized to lease nonexcess real property under the control of the department that is not needed for public use if the Secretary considers the lease to be advantageous to the United States and upon such terms that will promote the national defense or be in the public interest. The term of the lease may not be more than 5 years, unless the Secretary determines the term should be longer to promote the national defense or to be in the public interest. Lease payments shall be in cash or in-kind consideration for an amount not less than fair market value. In-kind consideration includes maintenance, protection, alteration, repair, or environmental restoration of property or facilities; construction of new facilities; providing facilities; or providing or paying for utility services.
DOD	Retention of Proceeds/ Leases of Non-Excess Property of Military Departments 10 U.S.C. § 2667	Proceeds from leases of a military department are deposited into a special account in the Treasury and are available to the Secretary of that military department for such activities as maintenance, protection, alteration, or environmental restoration of property or facilities; construction of new facilities; lease of facilities; or payment of utility services. At least 50 percent of the proceeds received shall be available for activities at the military installations where the proceeds are derived. Prior to fiscal year 2005, any amounts deposited in a special account from the disposition of property were subject to expenditure, as provided in an appropriation act. Beginning in fiscal year 2005, any amounts deposited into a special account from the disposition of property are appropriated and available for expenditure.[b]

Enclosure II. (Continued).

Real property holding agency	Authority	Description of authority
DOD	Conveyance of Damaged or Deteriorated Military Family Housing 10 U.S.C. § 2854[a]	The Secretary concerned is authorized to convey any family housing facility, including the real property associated with the facility, which due to damage or deterioration is in a condition that is uneconomical to repair. The person to whom the facility is conveyed shall pay an amount equal to the fair market value of the facility conveyed, including any real property conveyed along with the facility.[c]
DOD	Retention of Proceeds/ Conveyance of Damaged or Deteriorated Military Family Housing 10 U.S.C. § 2854[a]	Proceeds of any conveyance of a damaged or deteriorated military family housing facility shall be credited to the Department of Defense Housing Improvement Funds, 10 U.S.C. § 2883, and shall be available, without any further appropriation, to construct family housing units to replace the family housing facility conveyed under this section; to repair or restore existing military family housing; and to reimburse the Secretary concerned for the costs incurred by the Secretary in conveying the family housing facility.
DOD	Conveyance or Lease of Existing Property and Facilities 10 U.S.C. § 2878	The Secretary concerned is authorized to convey or lease property or facilities, including ancillary supporting facilities to eligible entities at such consideration the Secretary concerned considers appropriate for the purposes of the alternative authority for acquisition and improvement of military housing and to protect the interests of the United States.[d]
DOD	Retention of Proceeds/ Conveyance or Lease of Existing Property and Facilities 10 U.S.C. § 2883	Proceeds from the conveyance or lease of property or facilities under 10 U.S.C. § 2878 shall be credited to the Department of Defense Housing Improvement Funds. Proceeds may be used to carry out activities with respect to the alternative authority for the acquisition and improvement of military housing, including activities required in connection with the planning, execution, and administration of contracts subject to such amounts as provided in appropriation acts.

Real property holding agency	Authority	Description of authority
DOD	General Services Administration's (GSA) Disposal of Real Property Under a Military Department's Control that is Excess to the Department's Needs 40 U.S.C. § 572	The Administrator of GSA is authorized to dispose of property under the control of a military department that is not subject to closure or realignment and is excess to the department's needs.[e]
DOD	Retention of Proceeds/ GSA's Disposal of Real Property Under a Military Department's Control that is Excess to the Department's Needs 40 U.S.C. § 572	Proceeds from the disposition of the property are deposited into a special account in the Treasury, less expenses incurred by GSA for the disposition. Fifty percent of the proceeds are available for facility maintenance and repair or environmental restoration at the military installation where the property was located, and 50 percent of the proceeds are available for facility maintenance and repair or for environmental restoration by the military department that had jurisdiction over the property. Prior to fiscal year 2005, any amounts deposited into a special account from the disposition of property were subject to expenditure, as provided in an appropriation act. Beginning in fiscal year 2005, any amounts deposited in a special account from the disposition of property are appropriated and available for expenditure.[f]

Enclosure II. (Continued).

Real property holding agency	Authority	Description of authority
DOE	Leasing of Excess Property 42 U.S.C. § 7256	The Secretary of Energy is authorized to lease excess real property located at a DOE facility that is to be closed or reconfigured and is not needed by DOE at the time the lease is entered into if the Secretary considers the lease to be appropriate to promote national security or is in the public interest. The term of the lease may be up to 10 years, with an option to renew the lease for another 10 years, if the Secretary determines that a renewal of the lease will promote national security or be in the public interest. Lease payments may be in cash or in-kind consideration for an amount less than fair market value. In kind consideration may include services relating to the protection and maintenance of the leased property.
DOE	Retention of Proceeds/ Leasing of Excess Property 42 U.S.C. § 7256	To the extent provided in advance in appropriations acts, the Secretary is authorized to use the funds received as rents to cover administrative expenses of the lease, maintenance and repair of the leased property, or environmental restoration activities at the facility where the leased property is located.
GSA	Disposition of Real Property 40 U.S.C. § 543	The Administrator of GSA is authorized to dispose of surplus real property by sale, exchange, lease, permit, or transfer for cash, credit, or other property.
GSA	Conveyance of Property Consolidated Appropriations Act of 2005, P.L. No. 108-447, § 412, 118 Stat. 2809, 3259 (2004)	The Administrator of GSA, notwithstanding any other provision of law, is authorized to convey by sale, lease, exchange, or otherwise, including through leaseback arrangements, real and related personal property, or interests therein.

Real property holding agency	Authority	Description of authority
GSA	Retention of Proceeds/ Conveyance of Property Consolidated Appropriations Act of 2005, P.L. No. 108-447, § 412, 118 Stat. 2809, 3259 (2004)	Net proceeds from the disposition of real property are deposited in GSA's Federal Buildings Fund (FBF) and are used for GSA real property capital needs to the extent provided in appropriations acts.
NASA	Enhanced Use Lease Real Property Demonstration 42 U.S.C. § 2459j	The Administrator of NASA is authorized to enter into a lease agreement with any person or entity, including federal, state, or local governments, with regard to any real property at two NASA centers. The lease shall be for fair market value and payments may be in cash. Prior to December 31, 2008, NASA could have accepted for lease payments in-kind consideration such as construction, maintenance, or improvement of facilities, or providing services to NASA such as launch and payload processing services.[g]
NASA	Retention of Proceeds/ Enhanced Use Lease Real Property Demonstration 42 U.S.C. § 2459j	Cash consideration received for the lease is to be used to cover the full costs to NASA in connection with the lease and shall remain available until expended. Thirty-five percent of any remaining cash shall be deposited in a capital asset account available for maintenance, capital revitalization, and improvements of real property assets under the jurisdiction of the Administrator and shall remain available until expended. The remaining 65 percent of the cash shall be available to the respective center or facility engaged in the lease of nonexcess real property and shall remain available until expended for maintenance, capital revitalization, and improvements of real property assets at the respective center or facility, subject to the concurrence of the Administrator.

Enclosure II. (Continued).

Real property holding agency	Authority	Description of authority
NASA	Lease of Non-Excess Property 42 U.S.C. § 2459j	Effective December 31, 2008, the Administrator of NASA is authorized to enter into a lease agreement with any person or entity, including federal, state, or local governments, with regard to any nonexcess real property under the jurisdiction of the Administrator. The lease shall be for cash consideration of the fair market value as determined by the Administrator.[h]
NASA	Retention of Proceeds/ Lease of Non-Excess Property 42 U.S.C. § 2459j	Cash consideration received for the lease is to be used to cover the full costs to NASA in connection with the lease and shall remain available until expended. Thirty-five percent of any remaining cash shall be deposited into a capital asset account available for maintenance, capital revitalization, and improvements of real property assets under the jurisdiction of the Administrator and shall remain available until expended. The remaining 65 percent of the cash shall be available to the respective center or facility engaged in the lease of non-excess real property and shall remain available until expended for maintenance, capital revitalization, and improvements of real property assets at the respective center or facility, subject to the concurrence of the Administrator. Effective December 31, 2008, no funds may be used for daily operating costs.
State	Disposition of Property 22 U.S.C. § 300	The Secretary of State is authorized to sell, exchange, lease, or license any property or property interest acquired in foreign countries for diplomatic and consular establishments.

Real property holding agency	Authority	Description of authority
State	Retention of Proceeds/ Disposition of Property 22 U.S.C. § 300	Proceeds from the disposition of properties are applied toward acquisition, construction, or other purposes authorized by this chapter; Foreign Service Buildings; or deposited into the Foreign Service Buildings Funds, as in the judgment of the Secretary may best serve the government's interest.
USDA	Enhanced Use Lease Authority Pilot Program 7 U.S.C. § 3125a note[i]	The Secretary of Agriculture is authorized to establish a pilot program and lease nonexcess real property at the Beltsville Agricultural Research Center and the National Agricultural Library to any individual or entity, including agencies or instrumentalities of State or local governments, if the Secretary determines that the lease is consistent with, and will not adversely affect, the mission of the agency administering the property; will enhance the use of the property; will not permit any portion of the property or facility to be used for the public retail or wholesale sale of merchandise or residential development; will not permit the construction or modification of facilities financed by nonfederal sources to be used by an agency, except for incidental use; and will not include any property or facility required for any agency purpose without prior consideration of the needs of the agency. Consideration for any lease shall be for fair market value and for cash. The Secretary is authorized to enter into leases until June 18, 2013, and the term of the lease shall not exceed 30 years.
USDA	Retention of Proceeds/ Enhanced Use Lease Authority Pilot Program 7 U.S.C. § 3125a note	Consideration for leases shall be deposited in a capital asset account, which is available until expended, without further appropriation, for maintenance, capital revitalization, and improvements to the department's properties and facilities at the Beltsville Agricultural Research Center and the National Agricultural Library.

Enclosure II. (Continued).

Real property holding agency	Authority	Description of authority
USDA-Forest Service	Conveyance of Forest Service Administrative Sites 16 U.S.C. § 580d note[j]	The Secretary of Agriculture is authorized to convey administrative sites of 40 acres or less under the Secretary's jurisdiction by sale, lease, exchange, or combination of sale and exchange. An administrative site is defined as a facility or improvement, including curtilage, that was acquired or is used specifically for purposes of administration of the National Forest System (NFS); any federal land associated with a facility or improvement that was acquired or specifically used for purposes of administration of Forest Service activities and underlies or abuts the facility or improvement; or not more than 10 isolated, undeveloped parcels per fiscal year of not more than 40 acres each that were acquired or used for purposes of administration of Forest Service activities, but are not being so utilized such as vacant lots outside of the proclaimed boundary of a unit of NFS. This conveyance authority, which would have expired on September 30, 2008, was extended until March 6, 2009.[k]
USDA-Forest Service	Retention of Proceeds/ Conveyance of Forest Service Administrative Sites 16 U.S.C. § 580d note	Proceeds from the conveyance of administrative sites are available to the Secretary of Agriculture, until expended and without further appropriation, to pay any necessary and incidental costs in connection with the acquisition, improvement, maintenance, reconstruction, or construction of a facility or improvement for the NFS, and the conveyance of administrative sites, including commissions or fees for brokerage services.
USPS	Real Property Authorities 39 U.S.C. § 401(5)	The Postal Service is authorized to acquire in any legal manner, real property or any interest therein, as it deems necessary or convenient in the transaction of its business and to hold, maintain, sell, lease, or otherwise dispose of such property or any interest therein.

Real property holding agency	Authority	Description of authority
USPS	Real Property Authorities 39 U.S.C. § 401(6)	The Postal Service is authorized to construct, operate, lease, and maintain buildings, facilities, or equipment, and to make other improvements on any property owned or controlled by it.
USPS	Retention of Proceeds/ Real Property Authorities 39 U.S.C. §§ 2003 and 2401	Proceeds are deposited into the Postal Service Fund and remain available to the Postal Service without fiscal year limitation to carry out the purposes, functions, and powers authorized by Title 39, Postal Service. All revenues received by the Postal Service are appropriated to the Postal Service.
VA	Transfer Authority – Capital Asset Fund 38 U.S.C. § 8118	The Secretary of VA is authorized to transfer real property under VA's control or custody to another department or agency of the United States, to a state or political subdivision of a state, or to any public or private entity, including an Indian tribe until November 30, 2011. The property must be transferred for fair market value, unless it is transferred to a homeless provider. Property under this authority cannot be disposed of until the Secretary determines that the property is no longer needed by the department in carrying out its functions and is not suitable for use for the provision of services to homeless veterans by the department under the McKinney-Vento Act or by another entity under VA's EUL authority.
VA	Retention of Proceeds/ Transfer Authority 38 U.S.C. § 8118	Proceeds from the transfer of real property are deposited into the VA Capital Asset Fund and, to the extent provided in advance in appropriations acts, may be used for property transfer costs such as demolition, environmental remediation, and maintenance and repair; costs associated with future transfers of property under this authority; costs associated with enhancing medical care services to veterans by improving, renovating, replacing, updating, or establishing patient care facilities through minor construction projects; and costs associated with the transfer or adaptive use of property that is under the Secretary's jurisdiction and listed on the National Register of Historic Places.

Enclosure II. (Continued).

Real property holding agency	Authority	Description of authority
VA	Enhanced Used Leases 38 U.S.C. §§ 8161-8169	The Secretary of VA is authorized to enter into leases for up to 75 years with public and private entities for underutilized and unutilized real property that is under the Secretary's jurisdiction or control. EULs shall be for "fair consideration," (i.e., cash and/or in-kind consideration, such as construction, repair, or remodeling of department facilities); providing office space, storage, or other usable space; and providing good or services to the department. The authority to enter into EULs terminates on December 31, 2011.
VA	Retention of Proceeds/ Enhanced Use Leases 38 U.S.C. § 8165	Expenses incurred by the Secretary of VA in connection with EULs will be deducted from the proceeds of the lease and may be used to reimburse the account from which the funds were used to pay such expenses. The proceeds can be used for any expenses incurred in the development of additional EULs. Remaining funds shall be deposited into the VA Medical Care Collections Fund (see authority below for additional uses of EUL proceeds).
VA	Retention of Proceeds/ Enhanced Use Lease Property Consolidated Security, Disaster Assistance, and Continuing Appropriations Act of 2009, P.L. No. 110-329, § 213, 122 Stat. 3574, 3711 (2008)	At the Secretary's discretion, proceeds or revenues derived from EUL activities, including disposal, may be deposited into the "Construction, Major Projects" and "Construction Minor Projects" accounts and used for construction, alterations, and improvements of any VA medical facility.1

Real property holding agency	Authority	Description of authority
VA	Disposal of Enhanced Use Lease Property 38 U.S.C. § 8164	If the Secretary of VA determines during the term of an EUL or within 30 days after the end of the lease term that the property is no longer needed by the department, the Secretary is authorized to initiate an action to dispose of the property.
VA	Retention of Proceeds/ Disposal of Enhanced Use Lease Property 38 U.S.C. § 8165	Funds received by VA from a disposal of an EUL property are deposited into the VA Capital Asset Fund and may be used to the extent provided for in appropriations acts for property transfer costs such as demolition, environmental remediation, maintenance, and repair; costs associated with future transfers of property under this authority; costs associated with enhancing medical care services to veterans by improving, renovating, replacing, updating or establishing patient care facilities through construction projects; and costs associated with the transfer or adaptive use of property which is under the Secretary's jurisdiction and listed on the National Register of Historic Places (see authority below for additional uses of EUL disposal proceeds).
VA	Retention of Proceeds/ Disposal of Enhanced Use Lease Property Consolidated Security, Disaster Assistance, and Continuing Appropriations Act of 2009, P.L. No. 110-329, § 213, 122 Stat. 3574, 3711 (2008)	At the Secretary's discretion, proceeds or revenues derived from EUL activities, including disposal, may be deposited into the "Construction, Major Projects" and "Construction Minor Projects" accounts and used for construction, alterations, and improvements of any VA medical facility.

Source: GAO analysis.

Note: This list is not intended to be an all inclusive list of an agency's authorities. Furthermore, this list specifically excludes DOD authorities to sell or lease property under a base closure or realignment, lands managed by DOI or the Forest Service, except for

Forest Service administrative sites and the Agricultural Research Service's EUL pilot program, and transfers of individual properties authorized by Congress.

[a] Our review of DOD did not include real property at a military installation designated for closure or realignment under a base closure law. Therefore, for purposes of this appendix we have excluded DOD authorities relating to base closure or realignment. Additionally, while some authorities in this enclosure, such as 10 U.S.C. § 2667, contain subsections relating to base closure and realignment, for purposes of this enclosure we are referring to the other subsections of the statute.

[b] Department of Defense Appropriations Act of Fiscal Year 2005, P.L. No. 108-287, § 8034, 118 Stat. 951, 978 (2004).

[c] This authority does not apply to family housing facilities located at military installations approved for closure under a base closure law or family housing activities located at an installation outside the United States at which the Secretary of Defense terminates operations. See 10 U.S.C. § 2854a(a)(2).

[d] This authority does not apply to property or facilities located on or near a military installation approved for closure under a base closure law. See 10 U.S.C. § 2878(b).

[e] This authority does not apply to property at a military installation designated for closure or realignment pursuant to a base closure law. See 40 U.S.C. § 572(b)(2)(B)(ii).

[f] Department of Defense Appropriations Act of Fiscal Year 2005, P.L. No. 108-287, § 8034, 118 Stat. 951, 978 (2004).

[g] NASA was provided EUL authority in 2003. See the Consolidated Appropriations Resolution of FY 2003, P.L. No. 108-7, §418, 117 Stat. 11, 525-526 (2003).

[h] The Consolidated Appropriations Act for FY 2008, P.L. No. 110-161, § 533, 121 Stat. 1844, 1931-1932 (2007), amended NASA's EUL authority at 42 U.S.C. § 2459j to include any NASA non-excess real property, rather than just nonexcess real property at two NASA facilities. P.L. No. 110-161 also amended NASA's EUL authority at 42 U.S.C. § 2459j to allow for cash consideration only when entering into a lease and to prohibit any cash received for the EUL from being used for daily operating costs. These amendments are effective as of December 31, 2008.

[i] This pilot program was enacted in the Food, Conservation, and Energy Act of 2008, P.L. No. 110-246, § 7409, 112 Stat. 1651, 2014-2016 (2008).

[j] This authority, the Forest Service Facility Realignment and Enhancement Act, was enacted in 2005 as part of P.L. No. 109-54, Title V, §§ 501-505, 119 Stat. 499, 559-563 (2005).

[k] Consolidated Security, Disaster Assistance, and Continuing Appropriations Act of FY 2009, P.L. No. 110-329, §149, 122 Stat. 3574, 3581 (2008).

[l] This provision has been included in numerous appropriations acts. See the Consolidated Security, Disaster Assistance, and Continuing Appropriations Act of FY 2009, P.L. No. 110-329, § 213,110 Stat. 3574, 3711 (2008); the Consolidated Appropriations Act of FY 2008, P.L. No. 110-161, § 213, 121 Stat. 1844, 2270 (2007); the Consolidated Appropriations Act of FY 2005, P. L. No. 108-447, § 117, 118 Stat. 2809, 3293 (2004); and the Consolidated Appropriations Act of FY 2004, P.L. 108-199, § 117, 118 Stat. 3, 371 (2004).

ENCLOSURE III: FLOW CHARTS OF AGENCIES' REAL ESTATE DISPOSAL PROCESSES

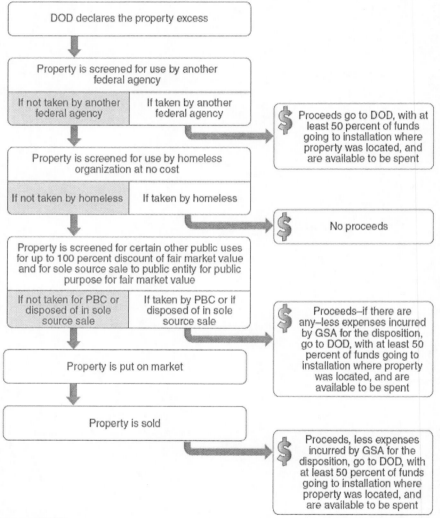

Source: DOD.
Note: This flow chart reflects the disposal process under 40 U.S.C. § 572.

Figure 9. DOD's Real Property Disposal Process.

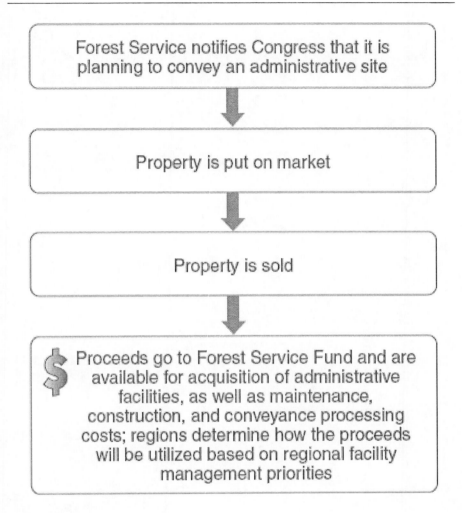

Source: USDA.

Figure 10. Forest Service's Real Property Disposal Process.

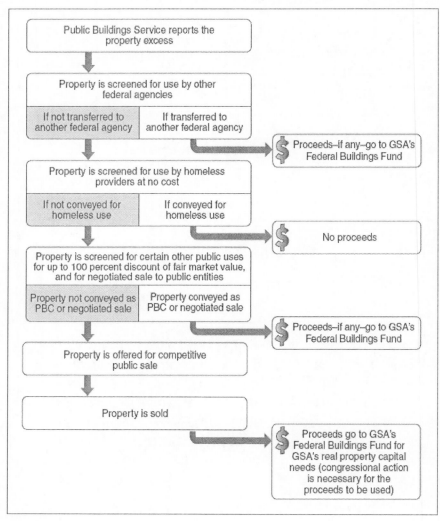

Source: GSA.

Figure 11. GSA's Process for Selling Excess GSA-Controlled Real Property.

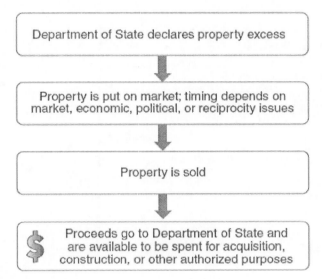

Source: State Department.

Figure 12. State Department's Real Property Disposal Process.

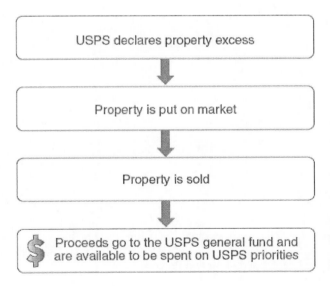

Source: USPS.

Figure 13. U.S. Postal Service's Real Property Disposal Process.

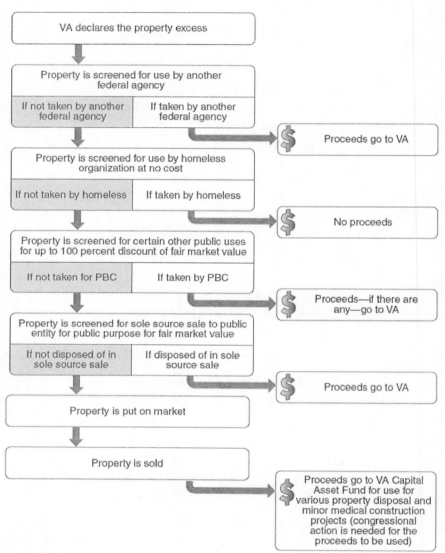

Source: VA.
Note: If sold by GSA, the proceeds are given to the U.S. Treasury.

Figure 14. VA's Real Property Disposal Process.

End Notes

[1] Section 102 of Title 40 of the United States Code defines "excess property" as property under the control of a federal agency that the federal agency determines is not required to meet the agency's needs or responsibilities. The General Services Administration's Federal Management Regulation defines "not utilized property" as an entire property or portion of a property that is not occupied for current program purposes of the accountable agency or property that is occupied in caretaker status only. The regulation defines "underutilized property" as an entire property or portion of a property that is used only at irregular periods or intermittently by the accountable agency or property that is being used for the agency's current program purposes that can be satisfied with only a portion of the property (41 C.F.R. §§102-75.45 & 75.50).

[2] GAO, *High-Risk Series: An Update,* GAO-03-119 (Washington, D.C.: January 2003) and *High-Risk Series: An Update,* GAO-09-271 (Washington, D.C.: January 2009).

[3] Executive Order No. 13327, Feb. 4, 2004.

[4] Under the BRAC process, the Secretary of Defense is authorized to close certain military bases and dispose of property. In the scope of our review, we included real property disposed of by DOD through its authority to convey or lease existing property and facilities outside of the BRAC process.

[5] Because USDA's Agricultural Research Service (ARS) received pilot authority to enter into EULs for certain properties effective June 2008, but had not entered into any EULs during our review, we did not include ARS in the scope of our review.

[6] DOI has authorities that permit it to sell certain real property and retain the proceeds, but we did not include lands managed by DOI in our review.

[7] According to State, committee reports accompanying State's appropriations acts routinely require the department to notify Congress through the reprogramming process of the specific planned use of the proceeds of the sale of excess property. Furthermore, State indicated that it routinely includes discussion of the use of proceeds from the sale of real property in its budget justifications and financial plans.

[8] VA has two authorities under which it can sell real property and retain the proceeds. Under the first authority, the Capital Asset Fund (CAF) at 38 U.S.C. § 8118, VA can sell real property subject to certain restrictions. The proceeds are deposited in the CAF which are subject to further congressional action. Under the second authority, VA can sell real property related to an EUL that is no longer needed by the department. When this property is sold, under 38 U.S.C. § 8165, the proceeds are deposited in the CAF which would require further congressional action. Alternatively, in its annual appropriations act, the Secretary of VA is authorized to deposit proceeds from EULs, including sale proceeds, into VA's major or minor construction accounts, and use these proceeds for construction, alteration, and improvement projects. While congressional action is needed to pass VA's annual appropriation acts, no further congressional action is needed for VA to spend these proceeds.

[9] Since these agencies lack disposal authority, GSA would dispose of these agencies' excess property and the proceeds from the disposal would be deposited into the U.S. Treasury.

[10] Land that DOD classifies as "underutilized" or "not utilized" may not necessarily be considered "excess property." Pursuant to 40 U.S.C. §102, "excess property" is defined as property under the control of a federal agency that the head of the agency determines is not required to meet the agency's needs or responsibilities. Therefore, a parcel of DOD real

property could potentially be underutilized, yet still not be excess, because it is required to meet certain DOD needs or responsibilities.

[11] Title 40 of the United States Code governs the disposal of most federal real property. When a federal agency no longer needs a property to carry out its mission responsibilities, the property is reported as excess and is offered to other federal agencies for use. If another federal agency does not have a need for the property, it is considered surplus to the federal government. Pursuant to the McKinney-Vento Homeless Assistance Act, the Department of Housing and Urban Development then reviews the property to determine if it is suitable for homeless use. If the property is considered suitable for homeless use, it is first made available for homeless use consideration at 100 percent discount of fair market value by state or local governments and certain tax-exempt nonprofit organizations for 60 days prior to any other public benefit uses. If the property is not considered suitable or if there is no interest in the property, it becomes available for other public benefit uses through the public benefit conveyance (PBC) program. In the PBC program, state or local governments and certain tax-exempt nonprofit organizations can obtain the property for an approved public benefit use, such as education or parks and recreation. Properties can be conveyed to grantees at a discount of up to 100 percent of fair market value.

[12] 10 U.S.C. §§ 2854a and 2878.

[13] DOD has several different authorities to retain proceeds from the sale of real property. Under 40 U.S.C. § 572, the Administrator of GSA is authorized to dispose of property under the control of a military department that is not subject to closure and is excess to the department's needs. Proceeds from the sale are deposited into a special account in the Treasury for DOD and, since fiscal year 2005, are available for expenditure without being subject to further congressional action. Also under 10 U.S.C. § 2854a, DOD is authorized to convey damaged or deteriorated military family housing and to retain the proceeds for use without further congressional action. Under 10 U.S.C. § 2878, the Secretary is authorized to convey property or facilities for the military housing privatization initiative and the use of the proceeds is subject to further congressional action.

[14] Under 40 U.S.C. § 113(e)(7), State is exempt from following Title 40 requirements regarding the sale of excess real property. Furthermore, because State's properties are located outside of the United States, the McKinney-Vento Homeless Assistance Act does not apply. USPS's own authorities also exempt USPS from these requirements. The Forest Service interprets its authority to convey administrative sites under 16 U.S.C. § 580d note to exempt it from the requirements under Title 40 of the United States Code and the McKinney-Vento Homeless Assistance Act.

[15] FRPP data are requested by constructed asset, and one "property" may include many constructed assets.

[16] Although we asked the agencies to provide data on the number of properties sold during fiscal years 2006 and 2007, we are not reporting them because the methods that the agencies used to count the number of properties were not comparable.

[17] 41 C.F.R. § 102-75.115.

[18] In a 2003 report, we found that outleasing historic properties under the National Historic Preservation Act, 16 U.S.C. § 470h-3, promotes certain benefits such as the restoration of historic buildings, but that it is unclear whether selling such properties would accomplish the same purpose with greater economic benefit to the taxpayer. See GAO, *Budget Issues: Alternative Approaches to Finance Federal Capital*, GAO-03-1011 (Washington, D.C.: Aug. 21, 2003). At times, these outleases, like some EULs, have been long-term leases for commercial development. For example, in Washington, D.C., GSA leased the U.S. Tariff

Building, which had been vacant for a number of years, to the Kimpton Hotel and Restaurant Group, Inc. for 60 years. This group restored the building, converting it into a luxury hotel.

[19] GAO, *Defense Infrastructure: Services' Use of Land Use Planning Authorities,* GAO-08-850 (Washington, D.C.: July 23, 2008).

[20] VA's CAF authority at 38 U.S.C. §8118 established a revolving fund and granted the Secretary the authority to transfer, sell, or exchange real property and deposit funds into the CAF. CAF funds may be used for property transfer costs, minor medical construction projects, or historic VA properties.

[21] Under 38 U.S.C. §8165, VA is authorized to spend EUL proceeds without further congressional action for EUL expenses and veterans' health care services. Additionally, in its annual appropriations act, the Secretary of VA is authorized to deposit EUL proceeds into VA's major or minor construction accounts, and use them for construction, alteration, and improvement projects. While congressional action is needed to pass VA's annual appropriation acts, no further congressional action is needed for VA to spend these proceeds.

[22] According to VA officials, VA also has a profit participation agreement for the EUL based on the lessee's net income. In 2007, VA received proceeds from the profit participation for the first time in the amount of about $32,000.

[23] GSA received permanent authority to sell and retain the net proceeds from real property sales in fiscal year 2005. Section 412 of P.L. No. 108-447, 118 Stat. 2809, 3259 (2004).

[24] Section 407 of P.L. No. 108-447, 118 Stat. 2809, 3258 (2004). Although we excluded from our legal research transfers of individual properties authorized by Congress, we visited this property upon GSA's recommendation.

[25] Under a historic easement, the future owner would have to obtain approval from the Maryland Historical Trust for any changes to the interior or exterior of the building.

[26] A USPS official said that the Postal Service originally agreed to sell the Farley building for $230 million, including $55 million in a deferred purchase price that will not be paid until the commercial component of the development is built. The official said that as of January 2009, USPS has received $195 million, which is $20 million more than was expected because of inflation and other factors.

[27] In 2001, the Forest Service received authority for a pilot program to convey excess Forest Service administrative structures and to retain the proceeds from those sales. This 2001 authority was replaced with its current authority in 2005.

[28] GAO, *NASA: Enhanced Use Leasing Program Needs Additional Controls,* GAO-07-306R (Washington, D.C.: Mar. 1, 2007).

[29] NASA indicated that the initial agencywide administrative policy, which was published in July 2007, has since been updated to reflect the legislation and changes to NASA's EUL authority. According to NASA, the most recent update was sent to all NASA centers in December 2008 and the agency's Office of the Chief Financial Officer sent out financial policy for EUL revenue in May 2008. NASA indicated that these actions were taken to address the concerns expressed in the GAO review and have ensured accountability and transparency and protection for the government.

[30] Under the BRAC process, the Secretary of Defense is authorized to close certain military bases and dispose of property. In the scope of our review, we included real property disposed of by DOD through its authority to convey or lease existing property and facilities outside of the BRAC process.

In: Federal Real Property Disposition   ISBN: 978-1-62100-048-8
Editor: Iain D. Haque   © 2012 Nova Science Publishers, Inc.

Chapter 6

ACQUIRING FEDERAL REAL ESTATE FOR PUBLIC USES[*]

General Services Administration Public Buildings Service

---

[*] This is an edited, reformatted and augmented version of a GSA Public Buildings Service publication.

Bell Federal Service Center

Bell, CA

Conveyed by GSA – March 29, 2007

Type of Conveyance – Homeless

Conveyed to – Salvation Army

Current Use – The property is being used for the receipt, storage, shipping and other warehouse-type activities of non food materials to support homeless persons assistance operations.

OVERVIEW

The mission of the General Services Administration (GSA) is to help federal agencies better serve the public by offering, at best value, superior workplaces, expert solutions, acquisition services, and management policies. GSA consists of the Federal Acquisition Service (FAS), the Public Buildings Service (PBS), and various other business lines dedicated to serving the needs of our customers.

PBS serves as the Federal Government's builder, developer, lessor, and manager of governmentowned and leased properties. PBS is the largest and most diversified real estate organization in the world.

The PBS Office of Real Property Disposal is responsible for managing the utilization and disposal of Federal excess and surplus real property government-wide.

As part of the disposal process, the Office of Real Property Disposal partners with other Federal Agencies to ensure that local communities are given the opportunity to benefit from surplus Federal real property by making it available for numerous public purposes. These opportunities have a lasting positive impact on communities, as the reuse of Federal Property can serve as an integral component of a community's vitality.

Homeless-assistance providers, eligible non-profit organizations, economic development entities, and state and local governments are generally given priority before surplus property is made available for sale to the general public.

New learning centers, transitional housing, expanded employment opportunities, revitalized waterfronts, rehabilitated historic properties, parks and open spaces are all essential to community growth and development.

When disposing of Federal real estate, the Office of Real Property Disposal follows a process mandated by Federal law and Executive Orders. This chart illustrates the various disposal methods (in order of progression) that may be utilized when finding the best possible use for surplus Federal property.

Excess

If a Federal agency no longer needs a property to carry out its program responsibilities, it reports this property as 'excess' to its needs.

Federal Transfer

GSA first offers excess property to other Federal agencies that may have a program need for it. If another Federal agency identifies a need, the property can be transferred to that agency.

Surplus Property

If there is no further need for the property within the Federal Government, the property is determined "surplus" and may be made available for other uses through public benefit conveyances (PBCs), negotiated sales, or public sales.

Negotiated Sale

GSA can negotiate a sale at appraised fair market value with a state or local government if the property will be used for another public purpose.

Public Sale

If state and local governments or other eligible non-profits do not wish to acquire the property, GSA disposes of surplus property via a competitive sale to the public.

Public Uses

After determining if the property is suitable to assist the homeless, GSA can make surplus Federal property available to public bodies (such as state and local governments or certain qualified tax exempt 501(c)(3) nonprofit institutions) through public benefit conveyances (PBCs) and/or negotiated sale based on the property's highest and best use.

Homeless Screening

If a property is suitable for homeless use (as determined by HUD), GSA must first consider transferring the property as a homeless conveyance before any other public benefit conveyance may be considered.

Public Benefit Conveyance (PBC)

As a PBC, the property can be substantially discounted in price (up to 100% of fair market value) if it is used for a specific public use that qualifies for a PBC through a partner sponsoring agency.

Types of Public Benefit Conveyances

Homeless
Education
Correctional
Emergency Management
Airports
Self-Help Housing
Park & Recreation
Law Enforcement
Wildlife Conservation
Public Health
Historic Monuments
Port Facilities
Highways
Negotiated Sale

U.S. Custom House & Post Office; St. Louis, MO

Conveyed by GSA– October 13, 2004

Type of Conveyance – Historic Monument

Conveyed to – Missouri Development Finance Board

Current Use – After a $35 million renovation, the building has an assortment of public businesses and services. They include Webster University's downtown campus, the Missouri Court of Appeals, a branch of the St. Louis public library, a restaurant, and a variety of state and private offices.

PUBLIC USES OF PROPERTY

Public uses for properties are those that are accessible to and can be shared by all members of a community. These uses include: community centers, schools and colleges, parks, municipal buildings, emergency management facilities, and many others. Homeless assistance groups, state and local governments, eligible non-profit organizations and other community-based institutions may apply for Federal property that is made available for public use.

There are three important and distinct aspects to the Public Benefit Conveyance Process: Homeless Assistance, Public Benefit Conveyances and Negotiated Sales.

HOMELESS ASSISTANCE

GSA is required to coordinate with the U.S. Department of Housing and Urban Development (HUD) to determine if surplus Federal property is suitable and/or available for use to assist the homeless as soon as it is declared 'surplus' to the Federal Government. If the property is suitable for homeless use, GSA must first consider homeless needs before any other public uses can be considered. Properties can be used to provide shelter, services, storage, or other uses which benefit homeless persons.

If properties are not suitable and/or available for homeless use, or if there is no interest in a homeless conveyance, GSA proceeds with the public benefit conveyance process working closely with its partner sponsoring agencies.

The McKinney-Vento Homeless Assistance Act (42 U.S.C. 11411) requires that public uses aimed at assisting the homeless are given top priority before other community uses are considered.

Mesa Federal Building; Mesa, AZ

Conveyed by GSA – August 2002

Type of Conveyance – Parks Conveyance

Conveyed to – City of Mesa

Current Use – The building is now used for 7the Mesa Southwest Museum Annex to display traveling exhibits from around the world. The museum features a multitude of exhibits representing southwest cultural and natural history. Visitors to the museum learn about the history of the state from prehistoric Arizona forward.

For more information, visit http://www.cityofmesa.org/swmuseum/.

PUBLIC BENEFIT CONVEYANCES

A public benefit conveyance (PBC) allows the Federal government to lease or transfer title of surplus property to qualified entities for public uses at a substantial discount (up to 100% of fair market value). The intent of a PBC is to support property uses that benefit the community as a whole.

A PBC can provide access to property for public and non-profit entities that may not otherwise be able to acquire it for community uses.

THE ROLE OF SPONSORING AGENCIES

All public benefit conveyances are sponsored by a designated Federal agency. While the decision to convey rests with GSA, the sponsoring agency serves as the approving authority that decides if the proposed use is a viable program (e.g., the National Park Service for park and recreation conveyances). These sponsoring agencies are responsible for reviewing the PBC application, educating the grantee on or about the conditions of the conveyance and, in some cases, deeding the property to the new owner. Either the Sponsoring agency or GSA periodically monitor properties conveyed for public benefit uses to ensure that the property continues to be used for the purpose for which it was conveyed.

TIMEFRAME FOR PBCS

Depending on the type of PBC, the use of the property that is conveyed can be restricted for up to 30 years or in perpetuity. If at any time the property is not used for its intended purposes, it may be returned to the Federal government. If the recipient of the property complies with the deed restrictions for the specified period, the use restriction will be lifted at the end of that time frame (except for those restrictions granted in perpetuity) and the grantee may use or sell the property for any purpose consistent with local land use regulations.

TYPES OF PBCS

To qualify for a PBC, eligible public entities and non-profit organizations must express interest in a property during the surplus screening process and apply to the specific sponsoring agency to acquire the surplus property for a particular public use. Below are descriptions of each qualifying PBC use, the required years of use, and the sponsoring agency.

Homeless Use

Agency: Department of Health & Human Services
Duration: 30 years
For: Use as facilities to assist the homeless. This also includes facilities used to assist the homeless as a permissible use in the protection of public health. Conveyance for homeless assistance has a priority of consideration over all other public benefit uses.

Educational Use

Agency: Department of Education
Duration: 30 years
For: School, classroom, or other educational uses.

Public Health

Agency: Department of Health & Human Services
Duration: 30 years
For: Use in the protection of public health, including research and hospitals.

Correctional Facility Use

Agency: Department of Justice
Duration: In perpetuity

For: Correctional facility use for the care or rehabilitation of criminal offenders.

Public Parks and Public Recreation Areas

Agency: Department of Interior, National Park Service
Duration: In perpetuity
For: Use as a public park or recreation area.

Historic Monuments

Agency: Department of Interior
Duration: In perpetuity
For: Historic preservation purposes. Historic federal properties such as courthouses, post offices, and military bases are conveyed under this program. These properties must be preserved in accordance with federal treatment standards, which allow rehabilitation for new uses, including revenueproducing activities.

Port Facilities

Agency: Department ofTransportation
Duration: In perpetuity
For: Development or operation of a port facility.

Highways

Agency: Department ofTransportation
Duration: No restriction
For: Federal or other highway or as a source of material for construction or maintenance of any highway adjacent to Federal real property.

Wildlife Conservation

Agency: GSA in consultation with the Department of Interior, Fish and Wildlife Service
Duration: In perpetuity
For: Wildlife conservation purposes or in support of the conservation of wildlife or the national migratory bird management program.

Law Enforcement

Agency: Department of Justice
Duration: In perpetuity
For: Control or reduction of crime and juvenile delinquency, enforcement of criminal law, investigative activities, forensic laboratory functions, or training.

Public Airports

Agency: GSA in consultation with the Federal Aviation Administration
Duration: In perpetuity
For: Development, improvement, operation, or maintenance of a public airport. This can include property needed to develop sources of revenue from non-aviation businesses at a public airport.

Self-Help Housing

Agency: Department of Housing & Urban Development
Duration: 30 years
For: Housing and/or housing assistance to low income individuals and families. Individuals and families receiving property under this authority are required to contribute a "significant" amount of labor toward the construction, rehabilitation, or refurbishment of the property.

Emergency Management

Agency: Federal Emergency Management Agency
Duration: In perpetuity
For: Emergency management response purposes, including fire and rescue services

Former Federal Building; Ruston, LA

Conveyed by GSA – 2007

Type of Conveyance – Correctional

Conveyed to – City of Ruston and Lincoln Parish Police Jury

Current Use – The main floor is fully occupied by PRIDE of Lincoln, Inc., Crime and Drug Prevention Program. Also on the main floor is the City and Parish Tax Collection office from which funds collected go to support the local Sheriff's office. Geographic Information Systems, located in the west offices, assists in dispatching correctional officials to sites in the City and Parish. The basement has recently been renovated to house the Sheriff's task force for computer solicitation.

QUALIFIED ENTITIES

Only certain entities are eligible to receive a public benefit conveyance. GSA and Federal sponsoring agencies can convey surplus Federal property through a PBC to state and local governments or for certain PBCs to qualified non-profit organizations.

ELIGIBILITY FOR NON-PROFIT ORGANIZATIONS

The general definition of a qualified non-profit organization is any institution, organization, or association that meets two main criteria:

- The net earnings of the organization must not benefit any private shareholder or individual.
- The organization must be determined by the Internal Revenue Service to be tax exempt under section 501(c)(3) of the IRS Code.

Qualification determinations are made in collaboration with GSA's Federal sponsoring agencies.

NEGOTIATED SALES

A negotiated sale is a transaction in which the Federal Government offers state and local governments the right to purchase property at appraised fair market value before it is offered to the general public. Property acquired via negotiated sale must be for a public purpose, although they are not restricted to a particular use.

Much like a public benefit conveyance, a negotiated sale can bring about substantial benefits for the local community and municipality. State or local governments can purchase a property before it is listed on the open market.

In most instances, localities save money by reusing Federal facilities and avoiding unnecessary expenses associated with building new structures.

Federal facilities can often be adapted to another public use without substantial rehabilitation costs. For example, a Federal courthouse may be easily retrofitted as a local courthouse facility.

Two general types of uses that typically qualify for a negotiated sale are direct public uses and economic development uses.

Direct Public Uses Examples

- Use of a Federal office building as a city municipal or administrative building.
- Development of a community center or public works depot.

Economic Development Examples

- Redevelopment of the land parcel as an industrial park.
- Subdivide the property, build streets and other infrastructure, and market the property at a later date.

Chet Holifield Federal Building

Parking Lot

Laguna Niguel, CA

Conveyed by GSA – May 13, 1999

Type of Conveyance – Negotiated Sale

Conveyed to – Laguna Niguel Community Services District Current Use – The property has since been converted from a parking lot into a skate and soccer park featuring a 20,000 square foot Skateboard Park and synthetic grass soccer field. This state of the art park provides year round enjoyment for soccer and skateboard enthusiasts. A variety of local teams play at the park and it is open to the general public for a low admission cost.

TIME FRAME FOR NEGOTIATED SALES

In addition to the public use requirement, negotiated sales include an "excess profits clause." If within a specified period of time following the negotiated sale the purchaser sells the property, all proceeds in excess of the original negotiated price (plus allowable expenses) will be returned to the Federal government. This clause was established to prevent localities from "land banking" property and then selling it for a higher price to a third party. After the designated period, the public entity is entitled to do as they wish with the property.

HOW TO FIND AVAILABLE FEDERAL PROPERTY

When surplus property becomes available as a possible PBC or negotiated sale, GSA prepares a surplus screening notice for the property. The notice contains a brief description of the property, lists the PBC uses and statutes under which the property can be conveyed, and contact information for the Regional GSA office and appropriate sponsoring agencies.

Surplus screening notices are available on the GSA Office of Real Property Disposal Resource Center at https://rc.gsa.gov. Public entities are encouraged to visit this website for valuable information regarding Federal properties and GSA regulations.

RESPONDING TO A SURPLUS SCREENING NOTICE

Eligible public entities interested in acquiring the surplus property must inform the appropriate GSA Regional office and Federal sponsoring agency in writing within 30 days of the date on the notice.

Interested parties should indicate:

1. The intended use of the property,
2. A reference to the applicable Federal statute or statutes that allow for the intended use of the property (see 'Authorizing Legislation' section of this book),
3. How much of the property is needed if the entire parcel is not desired,

4. The length of time that is required to develop and submit a formal application for the property, and

5. The reason for the time required developing and submitting a formal application.

Richland Federal Building

Parking Lot

Richland, WA

Conveyed by GSA– 2005

Type of Conveyance – Education

Conveyed to – Columbia Basin College

Current Use – The Health Sciences Center at Columbia Basin College will enable Columbia Basin College to double its nursing student capacity and build up programs including radiological studies and surgery technicians. The center opened it's doors in 2006. The new healthcare center will also meet the medical needs of the growing community.

Based upon the facts and circumstances involved, including the potential suitability of the property for the use proposed, the sponsoring agency will determine what constitutes a reasonable period of time to allow the interested party to develop and submit a formal application for the property. The sponsoring agency coordinates with GSA and the applicant throughout the process. The Sponsoring Agency performs final PBC application review, notifies the applicant of the decision, and provides further instructions for proceeding with the acquisition of the property.

PUBLIC SALES

If no interest from eligible public or non-profit entities is received within the specified time period, GSA concludes that there is no public benefit use for the property and proceeds with plans to market the property for competitive public sale. For more information on acquiring Federal property by public sale, please see our brochure, 'A Guide to Buying Federal Real Estate' or visit our website at www.propertydisposal.gsa.gov.

Columbia Federal Building

Columbia, MO

Conveyed by GSA– October 29, 2003

Type of Conveyance – Education

Conveyed to – YouZeum, formerly called the Health Adventure

Current Use – The YouZeum, formerly called the Health Adventure Center, was created by the Boone County Medical Society Alliance in the early 1990s. The mission of YouZeum is to provide an interactive environment where visitors can better understand the workings of the human body and the healthy choices they have within their control.

For more information, visit http://www.youzeum.org/.

AUTHORIZING LEGISLATION

The following Federal statutory language is provided for assistance in confirming an appropriate intended property use and in preparing a response to a surplus screening notice.

Educational Use

Title 40 U.S.C. 550(c) authorizes the Administrator of General Services, in his discretion, to assign to the Secretary of Education, as appropriate, for disposal of such surplus real property, including buildings, fixtures, and equipment situated thereon, as is recommended by the appropriate Secretary as being needed for school, classroom, or other educational uses. The Act authorizes the appropriate Secretary to sell or lease such properties to States or their political subdivisions and instrumentalities, and tax-supported educational institutions, nonprofit educational institutions, or other similar institutions not operated for profit which have been held exempt from taxation under section 501(c)(3) of the Internal Revenue Code of 1954, and to fix the sale or lease value of the property to be disposed of taking into consideration any benefit which has accrued or may accrue to the United States from the use of the property by any such State, political subdivision, instrumentality, or institution. The principal restrictive provision in the instrument of conveyance requires the property to be used continuously for a specified period for the specific purpose stated in the application for the property made to the Departments of Education.

Public Health Use

Title 40 U.S.C. 550(d) authorizes the Administrator of General Services, in his discretion, to assign to the Secretary of Health and Human Services, as appropriate, for disposal of such surplus real property, including buildings, fixtures, and equipment situated thereon, as is recommended by the appropriate Secretary as being needed for use in the protection of public health, including research purposes. The Act authorizes the appropriate Secretary to sell or lease such properties to States or their political subdivisions and instrumentalities, and tax-supported medical institutions, hospitals, or other similar institutions not operated for profit which have been held exempt from taxation under section 501(c)(3) of the Internal Revenue Code of 1954, and to fix the sale or lease value of the property to be disposed of taking into consideration any benefit which has accrued or may accrue to the United States from the use of the property by any such State, political subdivision, instrumentality, or institution. The principal restrictive provision in the instrument of conveyance requires the property to be used continuously for a specified period for the specific purpose stated in the application for the property made to the Department of Health and Human Services.

Public Parks and Public Recreational Areas

Title 40 U.S.C. 550(e) authorizes the Administrator of General Services, in his discretion, to assign to the Secretary of the Interior for disposal, such surplus property, including buildings, fixtures, and equipment situated thereon, as is recommended by the Secretary of the Interior as being needed for use as a public park or recreation area. The Act authorizes the Secretary to sell or lease such properties to any State, political subdivision, instrumentalities thereof, or municipality, and to fix the sale or lease value of the property to be disposed of, taking into consideration any benefit which has accrued or may accrue to the United States from the use of such property by any such State, political subdivision, instrumentality, or municipality.

Deeds conveying any surplus real property disposed of under this authority shall provide that the property shall be used and maintained for the purpose for which it was conveyed in perpetuity and may contain such additional terms, reservations, restrictions, and conditions as may be determined by the Secretary of the Interior to be necessary to safeguard the interest of the United States.

Historic Monuments

Title 40 U.S.C. 550(h) authorizes conveyance to any State, political subdivision, instrumentalities thereof, or municipality, of all the right, title, and interest of the United States in and to any surplus real and related personal property which in the determination of the Secretary of the Interior is suitable and desirable for use as a historic monument for the benefit of the public.

Conveyances of property for historic monument purposes under this authority shall be made without monetary consideration to the United States: Provided, that no property shall be determined under this authority to be suitable or desirable for use as an historic monument except in conformity with the recommendation of the National Park Advisory Board established under section 3 of the Act of Congress approved August 21, 1935 (16 U.S.C. 463) and only so much of any such property shall be so determined to be suitable or desirable for such use as is necessary for the preservation and proper observation of its historic features. Property conveyed for historic monument purposes may under certain circumstances be used for revenue producing activities to support the historic monument. All income exceeding the cost of repairs, rehabilitation, and maintenance shall be used for public historic preservation, park, or recreational purposes.

Deeds conveying any surplus real property under this authority shall be used and maintained for the purposes for which it was conveyed in perpetuity and may contain such additional terms, reservations, restrictions, and conditions as may be determined by the Administrator to be necessary to safeguard the interest of the United States.

Correctional Facility/Emergency Management Response Use

Title 40 U.S.C. 553 authorizes the Administrator of General Services, in his discretion, to transfer or convey to States, the District of Columbia, the Commonwealth of Puerto Rico, Guam, American Samoa, the Virgin Islands, the Trust Territory of the Pacific Islands, the Commonwealth of the Northern Mariana Islands, or any political subdivision or instrumentality thereof, surplus real and related personal property, without monetary consideration for:

1. Correctional facility purposes. The Attorney General must determine the surplus real and related personal property to be required for such purposes by an authorized transferee or grantee under an appropriate

    program or project for the care and/or rehabilitation of criminal offenders as approved by the Attorney General.

2. Law enforcement purposes. The Attorney General must determine the surplus real and related personal property to be required for any activity involving the control or reduction of crime and juvenile delinquency, or enforcement of the criminal law, including investigative activities, such as laboratory functions, as well as training.

3. Emergency management response purposes. The Directory of the Federal Emergency Management Agency must determine the surplus real and related personal property to be required for emergency management response purpose, including fire and rescue services.

The deed or other instrument of conveyance for property will require that all property be used and maintained for correctional facility, law enforcement, or emergency management response (including fire and rescue services) purposes in perpetuity and may contain such additional terms, reservations, restrictions, and conditions as may be determined by the Administrator to be necessary to safeguard the interest of the United States.

Port Facilities

Title 40 U.S.C. 554 authorizes the Administrator of General Services, in his discretion, to assign to the Secretary of Transportation for disposal, such surplus property, including buildings, fixtures, and equipment situated thereon, as is recommended by the Secretary of Transportation as being needed for the development or operation of a port facility. The Act authorizes the Secretary to convey properties at no cost to the States, the District of Columbia, the Commonwealth of Puerto Rico, Guam, American Samoa, the Virgin Islands, the Federated States of Micronesia, the Marshall Islands, and the Commonwealth of the Northern Mariana Islands, or any political subdivision, municipality, or instrumentality thereof. Deeds conveying any surplus real property disposed of under this authority shall be made without monetary consideration to the Federal Government and provide that the property shall be used and maintained for the purpose for which it was conveyed in perpetuity and may contain such additional terms, reservations, restrictions, and conditions as may be determined by the Secretary of Transportation to be necessary to safeguard the interest of the United States.

Public Airports

Title 49 U.S.C. 47151 authorizes the conveyance or disposal of all right, title, and interest of the United States in and to any surplus real property or personal property (exclusive of property the highest and best use of which is determined by the Administrator to be industrial) to any State, political subdivision, municipality or tax-supported institution without monetary consideration to the United States. Such property must be determined by the Secretary of Transportation to be suitable, essential, or desirable for development, improvement, operation, or maintenance of a public airport as defined in the Federal Airport Act, as amended (49 U.S.C. 1101) or reasonably necessary to fulfill the immediate and foreseeable future requirements of the grantee for development, improvement, operation, or maintenance of a public airport, including property needed to develop sources of revenue from non-aviation businesses at a public airport. This section provides specific terms, conditions, reservations, and restrictions upon which such conveyances or disposals may be made.

Wildlife Conservation

Title 16 U.S.C. 667b-d provides that, upon request, real property which is under the jurisdiction or control of a Federal agency and no longer required by such agency: (1) can be utilized for wildlife conservation purposes by the agency of the State exercising administration of the wildlife resources of the State wherein the real property lies or by the Secretary of the Interior; and (2) is valuable for use for any such purpose, and which, in the determination of the Administrator of General Services, is available for such use may, not withstanding any other provisions of the law, be transferred without reimbursement or transfer of funds (with or without improvements as determined by said Administrator) by the Federal agency having jurisdiction or control of the property to (a) such State agency if the management thereof for the conservation of wildlife relates to other than migratory birds, or (b) to the Secretary of the Interior if the real property has particular value in carrying out the national migratory bird management program. Any such transfer to other than the United States shall be subject to the reservation by the United States of all oil, gas, and mineral rights and to the condition that the property shall continue to be used for wildlife conservation or other of the above stated purposes or in the event it is no longer used for such purposes or in the event it is needed for national defense purposes title thereto shall revert to the United States.

Homeless Assistance

Title V of the McKinney-Vento Act, as amended (42 U.S.C. 11411), authorizes the identification and use of underutilized and unutilized property for use as facilities to assist the homeless as a permissible use in the protection of public health. The Secretary of Housing and Urban Development collects data on Federal properties and identifies those suitable to assist the homeless. The General Services Administration and the Department of Health and Human Services make suitable surplus properties available to private nonprofit organizations, units of local government, and States for use as facilities to assist the homeless. These properties are leased, deeded, or made available on an interim basis at no cost to approved homeless assistance providers. Federal land-holding agencies may lease/permit suitable underutilized property to approved homeless assistance applicants.

Self-Help Housing

Title 40 U.S.C. 550(f)(3) authorizes the Administrator of General Services to assign to the Secretary of Housing and Urban Development (Secretary) surplus real property, including buildings, fixtures, and equipment situated thereon, as is recommended by the Secretary as being needed for providing housing or housing assistance for low income individuals or families.

This amendment contains a "sweat equity" provision which requires that any individual or family receiving housing or housing assistance constructed, rehabilitated, or refurbished through the use of the property must contribute a significant amount of labor toward the construction, rehabilitation, or refurbishment.

The Secretary is authorized to sell or lease surplus real property for housing or housing assistance to any State, political subdivision, or instrumentality of a State, or any nonprofit organization existing for the primary purpose of providing housing or housing assistance for low-income individuals or families.

Highways

Title 23 sections 107 and 317 of the United States Code authorize the conveyance of lands, or interests in lands, owned by the United States, to any State for the purpose of interstate construction, reconstruction, improvement, maintenance, right of way or materials source. Property being conveyed for these uses must be requested by the Secretary of Transportation and must be authorized by the Secretary of the Department supervising the administration of such lands or the interests in such lands. The conveyance of such property shall be made to the state transportation department or such political subdivision thereof as its laws may provide, in the form of purchase, donation, condemnation or other form so long as it complies with the laws of the United States. Title 40 U.S.C. 1304(b) provides for the conveyance of lands or interest in such lands, with or without consideration, to such state or political subdivision for the purposes of highway, street or alley widening.

Negotiated Sales

Title 40 U.S.C. 545(b)(8) and(9) allows the Administrator of General Services to prescribe regulations to govern non-competitive disposals and contracts for disposals if the disposal will be to a state, territory, or possession of the United States or to a political subdivision of, or a tax-supported agency in, a state, territory, or possession, and the estimated fair market value of the property and other satisfactory terms of disposal are obtained by negotiation or otherwise authorized by law. Section 545(e)(A)(ii) requires an explanatory statement of the circumstances shall be prepared for each disposal by negotiation of real property that has an estimated fair market value in excess of $100,000.

The prepared explanatory statement shall be transmitted to the appropriate committees of Congress for concurrence or approval in advance of the disposal.

Important Websites

For additional information about the General Services Administration (GSA) log onto:
www.gsa.gov

For additional information about the Office of Real Property Disposal log onto:
https://propertydisposal.gsa.gov/Property/About/

To search for real property available for sale by the GSA log onto:
www.propertydisposal.gsa.gov

To access our online auction site log onto:
www.auctionrp.com

To search for additional Federal real property and personal property (e.g., furniture, equipment, autos) log onto: www.GovSales.gov

For additional information about acquiring Federal real estate for public uses log onto:
www.propertydisposal.gsa.gov/resourcecenter/

Office of Real Property Disposal Publications

For information about purchasing surplus federal real property:
A Guide to Buying Federal Real Estate

For information about real property available for sale by the GSA:
Real Estate Sales List

For information about acquiring Federal real estate for public uses:
Acquiring Federal Real Estate for Public Uses

For information about environmental issues that affect the real property disposal process:
Environmental Framework for Real Property Disposal

For information about the community benefits of federal real property reuse:
Measuring the Benefit of Federal Real Property Reuse

For information about GovSales.gov:
GovSales.gov: The Official Site to Buy US Government Property

For information about the Value Added Services program:
FAS RP

To Obtain Any of the Above Publications, Please Write to:

Office of Real Property Disposal
General Services Administraion
1800 F Street, NW
Washington, DC 20405

GSA REAL PROPERTY DISPOSAL ZONES

New England Region
General Services Administration
Office of Real Property Disposal (1PR)
10 Causeway Street
Boston, MA 02222
Telephone: 617-565-5700 • Fax: 617-565-5720

Southeast Sunbelt Region
General Services Administration
Office of Real Property Disposal (4PR)
401 West Peachtree Street
Atlanta, GA 30365
Telephone: 404-331-5133 • Fax: 404-331-272

Great Lakes Region
General Services Administration
Office of Real Property Disposal (1PRM-5)
230 South Dearborn Street
Chicago, IL 60604
Telephone: 312-353-6045 • Fax: 312-886-9480

Greater Southwest Region
General Services Administration
Office of Real Property Disposal (7PR)
819Taylor Street
FortWorth, TX 76102
Telephone: 817-978-2331 • Fax: 817-978-2063

Pacific Rim Region
General Services Administration
Office of Real Property Disposal (9PR)
450 Golden Gate Avenue
San Francisco, CA 94102
Telephone: 888-472-5263 • Fax: 415-522-3213

Northwest Artic Region
General Services Administration

Office of Real Property Disposal (9PRF-10)
400 15th Street, SW
Auburn, WA 98001
Telephone: 253-931-7547 • Fax:253-931-7554

National Capital Region
General Services Administration
Office of Real Property Disposal
7th & D Street, SW
Washington, DC 20407
Telephone: 202-205-2127 • Fax: 202-205-5295

Central Office
General Services Administration
Office of Real Property Disposal
1800 F Street, NW
Washington, DC 20405
Telephone: 202-501-0084 • Fax: 202-501-2520

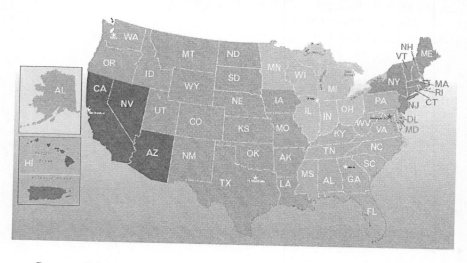

Smarter Solutions
Office of Real Property Disposal
Office of Real Property Asset Management
Public Buildings Service
U.S. General Services Administration

1800 F Street, NW
Washington, DC 20405
www.gsa.gov
09/2007

In: Federal Real Property Disposition   ISBN: 978-1-62100-048-8
Editor: Iain D. Haque   © 2012 Nova Science Publishers, Inc.

Chapter 7

A GUIDE TO BUYING
FEDERAL REAL ESTATE[*]

General Services Administration
Public Buildings Service

---

[*] This is an edited, reformatted and augmented version of a GSA Public Buildings Service
publication.

From Left to Right

Building: Isabella Ranger Administrative Site

Location: Isabella, MN

Estimated Acres: 2.5 Acres

Sales Method: Online Auction (2006)

Building: Hungry Horse Ranger Station

Location: Hungry Horse, MT

Estimated Acres: 37.232 Acres

Sales Method: Online Auction (2005)

Building: Carlsbad Federal Building

Location: Carlsbad, NM

Estimated Acres: 0.69 Acres

Sales Method: Online Auction (2006)

OVERVIEW

The mission of the General Services Administration (GSA) is to help federal agencies better serve the public by offering, at best value, superior workplaces, expert solutions, acquisition services, and management policies. GSA consists of the Federal Acquisition Service (FAS), the Public Buildings Service (PBS), and various other business lines dedicated to serving the needs of our customers.

PBS serves as the Federal Government's builder, developer, lessor, and manager of governmentowned and leased properties. PBS is the largest and most diversified real estate organization in the world.

The PBS Office of Real Property Disposal is responsible for managing the utilization and disposal of Federal excess and surplus real property government-wide.

Surplus Federal properties that are not conveyed to state/local governments and other eligible recipients are sold to the public through a competitive bidding process.

How Do I Find and Buy Federal Real Estate?

There are three easy steps to finding and buying surplus Federal real estate through GSA's Office of Real Property Disposal. As in any real estate transaction, bidders participate in an open, competitive market for the best purchase price.

STEP 1 – FIND AVAILABLE REAL ESTATE

Property Disposal Websites

GSA publishes current and upcoming public sales information on its FREE website: www.propertydisposal.gsa.gov.

The website features a US map which allows users to search for properties by state and type. Additional federal properties can also be found at www.govsales.gov --the official site to buy U.S. government property from various Federal agencies.

From Left to Right

Building: Middle River Station

Location: Baltimore, MD

Estimated Acres: 50 Acres

Sales Method (Year): Online Auction (2006)

Building: Federal Building, 517 Gold

Location: Albuquerque, New Mexico

Estimated Acres: 1 Acre

Sales Method (Year): Sealed Bid (2007)

Building: Mystic River Station

Location: Rapid City, SD

Estimated Acres: 8.25 Acres

Sales Method: Online Auction (2007)

Regional Offices

If you do not have access to the internet, the regional GSA office responsible for available property in your state can provide additional information. Contact information for each regional office is available on the inside back cover of this brochure.

Mass Media

GSA publicizes many of our public sales through advertisements and announcements in local and national newspapers, trade publications, and on radio and television.

STEP 2 – OBTAIN AN INVITATION FOR BID

GSA provides all the information necessary to bid on a particular property in the Invitation for Bid (IFB) package. You can obtain an IFB for a specific property from **https://www.propertydisposal.gsa.gov** or by calling the applicable GSA regional office.

IFB packages generally include the following information:

- location of the property
- property description
- maps
- pictures
- zoning and land use regulations
- environmental conditions
- general terms of the sale
- directions to the property
- Inspection guidelines

Other important information in the IFB includes official bid forms, instructions on the bidding process (not all properties are sold in the same manner), and the contact information for the GSA Project Manager responsible for the sale. If you have specific questions not addressed in the IFB, contact the assigned GSA Project Manager.

YOU MUST HAVE AN IFB TO BID ON A PROPERTY!

From Left to Right

Building: Thaddeus J. Dulski Federal Building

Location: Buffalo, NY

Estimated Acres: 1.5 Acres

Sales Method (Year): Online Auction (2006)

Building: Naval Medical Center-Oak Knoll

Location: Oakland, CA

Estimated Acres: 167 Acres

Sales Method (Year): Online Auction (2005)

Building: Union Station Air Rights

Location: Washington, DC

Estimated Acres: 14.96 Acres of air rights

Sales Method (Year): Sealed Bid (2005)

STEP 3 – BID ON REAL ESTATE

GSA has three commonly used methods for conducting public sales of surplus Federal real property (online auction, public auction, and sealed bid). In each, if the highest bid is acceptable and represents the fair market value of the property, an award is usually made. GSA reserves the right to act in the Government's best interest when reviewing all bids. Therefore, the highest bid may not always be accepted.

Online Auction

Properties available via online auction are advertised on the internet at www.auctionrp.com and www.govsales.gov. An online auction allows the bidder to conduct all bidding activities, including submitting the bid deposit and increasing bids, online. Bidders bid against each other on the website until a designated date. The highest bidder is declared once the auction officially closes.

Public Auction

Public auctions are conducted in a conventional "live outcry" auction setting with an auctioneer at a specific date and time. Bidders register, submit the bid deposit, and bid openly against each other until the highest bidder is declared.

Sealed Bid

Bidders mail in bids and bid deposits to the specified GSA regional office prior to the designated bid opening date and time. All bids are publicly opened on the bid opening date. After the public opening, no bids may be modified. The highest bidder is declared shortly after the auction officially closes.

The IFB package distributed for a particular property will indicate all bidding procedures and any special conditions that apply regarding the sale of the property. *Bidders should carefully inspect the property being offered for sale prior to bidding.* Properties are sold on an "as is, where is" basis. All bids are final once submitted.

GENERAL BIDDING GUIDELINES

Financing

Bids to purchase must be on an ALL CASH basis. Government credit terms are not available and GSA does not offer financing. Buyers are expected to arrange their own financing and to pay the balance in full by the closing date. After the date of acceptance, there is generally a 30- to 60-day period in which to send the final payment to close the sale.

Bid Deposit

An initial bid deposit is required to bid on a property. After acceptance of an offer, an additional deposit (usually equaling 10% of the sale price) may be required. The additional deposit may also be a fixed dollar amount rather than a percentage of the sale price. For those who are not the winning bidder, GSA will return deposits as soon as possible after the auction has ended. Bidders should refer to the IFB for specific terms and conditions.

Initial Bids

A minimum opening bid is usually suggested. Details about submitting an initial bid and additional bid increments can be found in the IFB package.

Selling Price

GSA strives to get the best value for the government by selling properties at fair market value. GSA does not sell federal real estate at discounted prices to the general public.

Important Websites

For additional information about the General Services Administration (GSA) log onto:
www.gsa.gov

For additional information about the Office of Real Property Disposal log onto:
https://propertydisposal.gsa.gov/Property/About/

To search for real property available for sale by the GSA log onto:
www.propertydisposal.gsa.gov

To access our online auction site log onto:
www.auctionrp.com

To search for additional Federal real property and personal property (e.g., furniture, equipment, autos) log onto: www.GovSales.gov

For additional information about acquiring Federal real estate for public uses log onto:
www.propertydisposal.gsa.gov/resourcecenter/

Office of Real Property Disposal Publications

For information about purchasing surplus federal real property:
A Guide to Buying Federal Real Estate

For information about real property available for sale by the GSA:
Real Estate Sales List

For information about acquiring Federal real estate for public uses:
Acquiring Federal Real Estate for Public Uses

For information about environmental issues that affect the real property disposal process:
Environmental Framework for Real Property Disposal

For information about the community benefits of federal real property reuse:
Measuring the Benefit of Federal Real Property Reuse

For information about GovSales.gov:
GovSales.gov: The Official Site to Buy US Government Property

For information about the Value Added Services program:
FAS RP

To Obtain Any of the Above Publications, Please Write to:

Office of Real Property Disposal
General Services Administration
1800 F Street, NW
Washington, DC 20405

GSA REAL PROPERTY DISPOSAL ZONES

New England Region
General Services Administration
Office of Real Property Disposal (1PR)
10 Causeway Street
Boston, MA 02222
Telephone: 617-565-5700 • Fax: 617-565-5720

Southeast Sunbelt Region
General Services Administration
Office of Real Property Disposal (4PR)
401 West Peachtree Street
Atlanta, GA 30365
Telephone: 404-331-5133 • Fax: 404-331-2727

Great Lakes Region
General Services Administration
Office of Real Property Disposal (1PRM-5)
230 South Dearborn Street
Chicago, IL 60604
Telephone: 312-353-6045 • Fax: 312-886-9480

Greater Southwest Region
General Services Administration
Office of Real Property Disposal (7PR)
819Taylor Street
FortWorth, TX 76102
Telephone: 817-978-2331 • Fax: 817-978-2063

Pacific Rim Region
General Services Administration
Office of Real Property Disposal (9PR)
450 Golden Gate Avenue
San Francisco, CA 94102
Telephone: 888-472-5263 • Fax: 415-522-3213

Northwest Artic Region
General Services Administration

Office of Real Property Disposal (9PRF-10)
400 15th Street, SW
Auburn, WA 98001
Telephone: 253-931-7547 • Fax:253-931-7554

National Capital Region
General Services Administration
Office of Real Property Disposal
7th & D Street, SW
Washington, DC 20407
Telephone: 202-205-2127 • Fax: 202-205-5295

Central Office
General Services Administration
Office of Real Property Disposal
1800 F Street, NW
Washington, DC 20405
Telephone: 202-501-0084 • Fax: 202-501-2520

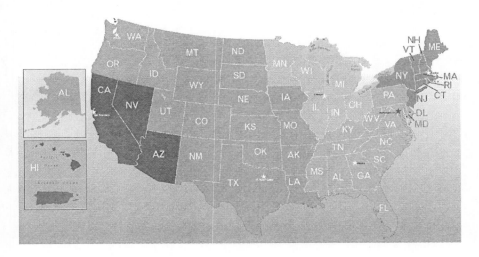

Smarter Solutions
Office of Real Property Disposal
Office of Real Property Asset Management
Public Buildings Service
U.S. General Services Administration

1800 F Street, NW
Washington, DC 20405
www.gsa.gov
09/2007

INDEX

D

E

F